Between the Bells is pu

John Paul Lederach, Pr
Peacebuilding, KROC I.........., University of Notre Dame

I have spent all of my life in and around Corrymeela, and nothing I have read has conveyed the hilarity, the challenge, the confusion, the mistakes and the miraculous depth of 'christian' community so truthfully or so clearly. This is the inside story. They are Paul's stories and stories about Paul, and they are stories that all of us who have been part of that curious community at the 'lumpy crossing' already know, but have not spoken.

> *Non Clamor, sed Amour, psalit in aure Dei.*
> (Not noise, but love, makes music in the ears of God.)
> *Thirteenth-century Catholic liturgy*

I can find no way to put it more succinctly.

Dr Duncan Morrow, Professor in Politics and Director of
Community Engagement, Ulster University

A more timely book could not be imagined. What is reconciliation in a non-heroic mode? How may the peace that passes all understanding be lived as a stumbling, daily, grace-filled practice? How may we learn that both these things are true: 'we are not enough' and 'together we are enough'? We are in the heart of conflict every day: how can we pray *large*, attentive to complex feelings toward others? How may we risk a 'multi-storied world' where what we cherish may be disparaged? Paul Hutchinson's artful storytelling animates these and many more questions. His stories take the reader onto holy ground: today I place before you blessing and curse. Choose blessing so that you may live.

Dr Alyda Faber, Associate Professor of Systematic Theology and
Ethics, Atlantic School of Theology, Nova Scotia

Between the Bells engages with important questions about living with conflict and working toward reconciliation. We are invited to consider how to live well with difference, to find ways to balance a person's past with curiosity about their future, to regularly 'recite the words of an alien, an outsider, a foreigner'.

The stories – difficult, funny, poignant – are all told with great humanity, wry self-awareness, and an insight which challenges us to question our own certainties.

Between the Bells tells of grief and loss and brokenness, yet offers hope. We are reminded again and again that 'We are never enough ... Together we are enough'.

We are called to attend to the details of everyday life: the blessing of holding an old man's hand, the inquiring mischievousness of small children.

The book is written in language that is both lyrical and everyday, offering insights that are accessible yet profound.

Between the Bells should be on the 'must-read' list of anyone interested in conflict, community, and reconciliation.

Diana Ginn, Schulich School of Law, Dalhousie University

In this book, Paul Hutchinson gives us a glimpse inside the patient, painstaking process of reconciliation that has been pioneered at Corrymeela. At times humorous, at other times harrowing, Hutchinson's stories are ultimately tales of hope in humanity.

Dr Gladys Ganiel, Research Fellow, Senator George J. Mitchell Institute for Global Peace, Security and Justice, Queen's University Belfast

Fantastic: written with humour and insight ... but look out for the punch.

Reconciliation is something for all of us, if it is to be real, lasting and embraced by wider society, challenging though that is.

The relational elements of real reconciliation practice are hard, not soft, and these stories make this clear – they bring a gritty quality to the reader.

I could identify so well with these Centre Director stories and encounters but I could never write them so sharply, so entertainingly and in such a challenging manner.

The sad thing is that too many people expect reconciliation to be the big-screen wonder story – something beyond the actions of ordinary people.

In fact, these stories remind us that the way to promote a more open and reconciled society is to see that in each encounter we have there is the possibility of: the unexpected breakthrough in understanding; the open hand when before there only has been a closed fist; the surprise that we, or the other, or both of us, regain some part of our lost humanity and our ability to be compassionate.

Reconciliation, potentially, is in the daily human encounters we each have, if we are able to see the wonder and life-changing moments these might be for us and these stories make this crystal clear, if we have open eyes to see this with.

Dr Derick Wilson, Reader Emeritus in Education, Ulster University

Paul Hutchinson's storytelling is compelling and honest. The reader is right there in the midst of an intimate moment, whether it is a symbolic handshake or sitting with a dying colleague. Paul's turn of phrase and poetic imagery is both delightful and thought-provoking at the same time, inviting the reader into the complexity of one's own history and experience.

How to explain what happens at Corrymeela, that Centre for Reconciliation in Northern Ireland? How to talk about complicated issues like forgiveness and the struggle to balance mercy and justice? How to challenge our quick judgements about who's good, who's bad, who's in or out, who's welcome or not? How to discover Jesus in the hell of hatred, bombs and murder? How to honestly affirm that we are, all of us, beloved by God?

Well, if you're Paul Hutchinson you don't lecture, write an essay or sermonize. Rather, you ground yourself in the lives of real, everyday people, who both challenge and surprise you. You tell stories, theirs and yours, and spin modern parables ...

Paul's stories captivate you and draw you into a different world, where you listen more carefully, and find yourself filled with new questions, with renewed curiosity and an openness to unexpected endings. You experience a brief, lived moment of reconciliation, an encounter with the Holy. And you realize you've just tasted what Corrymeela really means.

The Revd Gary Paterson, St Andrew's Wesley United Church; former Moderator of United Church of Canada

Paul Hutchinson is a man, a mediator, an artist, a father and a friend, whose observations are precise and provocative. He works and lives in a way that means encounters with him are imprinted within you. When Paul asked me to read his writing on reconciliation I was both curious and cautious. I knew my eyes would see delicate, intricate layers of meaning and that my heart would be tested. I had just reached 'encounter' and was already watching with trepidation as the social conventions of class and gender met reconciliation with refusal. Anger and sorrow reached out from that story and said: to know reconciliation is to know these feelings. Paul is a writer you encounter. By the end of this book, you will know the work of reconciliation in your being.

Mary Lynch, Director, Mediation Northern Ireland

Paul Hutchinson's writing is like the rest of his work: funny amidst the pain of life; self-deprecating, not falsely humble; brilliantly skilled but inviting; alive to the magic and the murk in everyday moments. Magic and murk have nowhere else to happen but the everyday, of course; cruelty and redemption too. This book is a gift to *anyone* who has ever sat down at the end of a hard day's body-draining courage, but now the dishes need to be done; or who is giving their life to the common good and has seen the mountaintop but sometimes struggles to get out of bed in the morning; who knows that there is more beauty than horror in the world, but doesn't always believe it. It's a book we need right now.

Gareth Higgins, Founding Director, Wild Goose Festival and Movies & Meaning; Editor, The Porch Magazine

Between the Bells

Stories of Reconciliation from Corrymeela

Paul Hutchinson

Foreword by Pádraig Ó Tuama

CANTERBURY
PRESS
Norwich

© Paul Hutchinson 2019

First published in 2019 by the Canterbury Press Norwich
Editorial office
3rd Floor, Invicta House
108–114 Golden Lane
London EC1Y 0TG, UK
www.canterburypress.co.uk
Canterbury Press is an imprint of Hymns Ancient
& Modern Ltd (a registered charity)

Hymns Ancient & Modern® is a registered trademark of
Hymns Ancient & Modern Ltd
13A Hellesdon Park Road, Norwich,
Norfolk NR6 5DR, UK

Scripture quotations are from The Holy Bible, New
International Version, Grand Rapids, MI: Zondervan, 1984.

British Library Cataloguing in Publication data

A catalogue record for this book is available
from the British Library

978 1 78622 076 9

Typeset by Regent Typesetting Ltd
Printed and bound in Great Britain by
CPI Group (UK) Ltd

Contents

Foreword by Pádraig Ó Tuama   xi
Introduction   xv

Soundings   1
Thanks   3
Mobile   8
Broken   10
When?   12
Seven contracts   14

Groundings   23
One.   25
Two.   38
Three.   43

The heart translated   45
What's in a word?   47
It's a beautiful day   52
Building a new heart   58
Dreams (Part 1)   59
Dreams (Part 2)   67
Blindfolding an Iraqi   71
Cowboy in the Croí   79
Ark in the heart   81

Together   87
01. Devotions   87
02. Good practice   88
03. Cameroon   88
04. A list of names   89
05. Where is the Jew?   91
06. Pure   97
07. Yael   98
08. Welcome to community   100
09. A Parable   106
10. Lift   107
11. Happy Monday   108
12. Apart (a part)   113

Encounter   115
01. Handshake   115
02. David   118
03. Plastic bag   121
04. Country kids   124
05. From on high   131
06. Covering   134
07. Past   136
08. Here, son   140
09. Notice   143
10. Limits   144

Coda   149

References   151

for the welcomed wild-cats

Roobers

Trolls

Binky

Tara

Tripod

Moon

Kiko

Rusty

Riffles

Ninio

Tiny Bob

Todd

Foreword

by Pádraig Ó Tuama

I have known Paul Hutchinson for many years. I have known and loved Paul Hutchinson for many years. I have known and loved and respected Paul Hutchinson for many years. When I was starting out in conflict mediation, he was already well practised in conflict mediation. We both liked poetry, stories, and were drawn – as conflicted men – to friendship and to places of conflict. I loved how he worked: with a presence that at once engaged and also maintained a distance for wonder. I saw him mediate difficult differences and I wanted to learn from him.

I learnt a lot.

Sometimes Paul would get me to come and give a talk to a group of people. Having a Catholic and a Protestant speak politics, religion and art with each other, and with groups, was important. He called me the Silky Tongued Fenian. I called him the Lippy Prod. One time, in a queue, a participant in a group came up and gave Paul a piece of his mind. The participant was Unimpressed with Paul. Paul stood. He listened. We were waiting for our food (Spaghetti Bolognese). Paul listened while he was shouted at. I thought of how much I wanted to shout at the person shouting at Paul. The shouting person had things to say. And said them. Loudly, and then left.

Paul turned to me. I could see he was hurt. I could see he was trying to hold it together. 'Everything is information, Pádraig' he said.

Earlier on that night Paul had been involved in a car-crash. Someone hadn't seen him and had bumped the side of his car. His car was damaged. He was shook up. He had been shook up and was holding it all together while he listened to the person who had things to say. He gave them space while his back ached, and while he was trying to process everything that a car-crash meant. This is not easy. He could have said: 'I was in a car crash, and this is hard to hear.' He could have said, 'Shut up.' But he didn't. He said, 'I'll need a little time to think.'

Everything is information.

Community is not a noun. It is not a thing. It is not a person, or a thing or a place – even if the place is beautiful. Community is a verb; it is a constant conjugation: of people with people; of people's politics with other people's politics; of religious conviction with other religious convictions; of griefs that seem to deground the griefs of others.

If my hurt is real, then yours can't be.

Then community happens and we realize that hurts circle round hurts. Hearts circle round hearts. People form unexpected relationships with each other. The world turns a little, we see something new made out of the nothing in between us. Community is conjugated, and it is as fragile and temporary as any verb.

Some religious communities centre around the call to prayer, or the call to a specific place. Corrymeela is called to witness to community in the messy place that happens when people hurt people. Corrymeela is located in a jurisdiction where questions of Irishness and Britishness, colonialism and land-rights, language and change have been located for 700 years. Many generous British and

Irish people have died in those centuries while the civic discord of our political relationships with each other raged.

Corrymeela does not shout out loud about peace. Corrymeela is not located at the place of discord like a diagnostician pointing purely to the way things should have been done. Corrymeela is there as an attempt to witness what it's like to tell the story of the hurt we've caused, the hurt we've lived, the hurt we're trying to tell. Community is also confession: in the face of sectarianism, we find ourselves noting our sectarianisms.

I remember once getting a curt email reply from Paul. Like I said, I've loved and admired Paul for years, and I'd asked his thoughts and got a reply that hurt. It didn't wreck things, but it did bother things. It stayed with me for days, and I wanted to get over it, but I couldn't. So, I wrote to him. My email was short, simple and also said: 'I can't stop thinking about that curt reply last week.' Paul's reply was simple. 'I can be so damned blunt sometimes. Sorry.'

I've been the leader of Corrymeela for five years now. The demands are endless. Like many jobs of leadership, one day can bring a governance demand, a fundraising demand, a private demand, a possibility of a resignation, the aching need for a deeper peace in our society, a complaint, an impossible demand, an insulting demand, a story you'll never forget, a story that you want to pause and listen to, a need in your family, a dozen disappointments, and double. I have repeated to myself every day his kind, simple, honest recognition of the way good people can hurt good people. To be in community is to be faced – over and over – with the need for acknowledgement and apology and forgiveness. Words matter in this project: and Paul's words are ruthless in their truth-telling, especially about himself.

Rumi said, in his poem 'The Great Caravan': 'Out beyond ideas of wrongdoing and rightdoing, there is a field; I'll meet you there.' Paul's writing is an echo of Rumi's intuition. Often in these stories he is holding conflict things together: the desire for reconciliation together with the desire for revenge; the hope for connection with the harm of conflict; the vocation of being a peacemaker with the vocation of being a spouse and parent; energy with exhaustion; calm with chaos; insight with incapacity. The field that Rumi invites us to is a field that has its own gifts and complicities. To enter into that field might feel like faithlessness to the story you've survived. That's okay – you don't have to go. But Paul's intuition – and the gift he brought to his time of leadership in Corrymeela – was that some important things can be discovered when we discover each other in this field.

At the heart of this book is a place called the heart – the Croí (pronounced *kree*). The Croí at Corrymeela is a building – the only building without a big window looking out to the sea and to Rathlin Island and to Scotland. It is a space for reflection, prayer, argument, anger, silence and noise. It has functioned as everything from chapel to changing room, and is a space where the ordinariness of surviving conflict is honoured. Hostility and hospitality are welcomed in the Croí. Paul's writing, too, in both its content and form, is a practice of hospitality. He is an artist, with deft skill in language, storytelling and writing. And he is also hungry, asking for the nurture of listening. He is vulnerable, and dexterous. For years, my life has been shaped by the presence of Paul's friendship and skill. Now yours is too.

Pádraig Ó Tuama
Feast of St Valentine, 2019

Introduction

Here is a popular image of reconciliation.

A man on a white horse is tasked by those with state power (who live in the centre of society) to ride out to the margins of society to deal with a conflict manifesting there. When successful, the man trots from the margins to the middle, applauded and lauded on his return. In this image, reconciliation is carried out by 'experts', by heroes, by the chosen few.

For me, this is a jarring image of reconciliation. Why?

It assumes that only men are allowed to sit on the white horse.

It assumes that conflict is always on the margins of society.

It assumes that there is no conflict in the middle or centre of society.

It assumes a lack of connection between margin and middle.

It assumes that a white horse is always required, i.e. that reconciliation can only be carried out in a 'heroic' mode, which excludes most of life, most lives.

It assumes that reconciliation is a 'one-time' thing, where an epic campaign can fix conflict in a short space of time.

I believe this is a distorted, exclusivist, disabling image of reconciliation.

But are there other images of reconciliation?

I will try to deepen that question by telling stories, stories about a place called Corrymeela.

Corrymeela is an open Christian community committed to reconciliation (www.corrymeela.org). Founded in 1965 by Ray Davey, in a Northern Ireland before the armed conflict known as the Troubles began. Gaining local and international recognition during the Troubles, gathering both Protestants and Catholics together for encounter, learning, residentials, temporary safe haven. Corrymeela is a 100-bed residential centre at Ballycastle, on a six-acre site, situated on a cliff overlooking the sea. It is a 'living community' of staff, volunteers and community members. Corrymeela is also a dispersed community of 160 members, mostly from around the north of Ireland, all committed to reconciliation wherever they live and work.

Corrymeela asks these questions:

What needs to be reconciled in the twenty-first century?

What has religion to offer in a positive way to Northern Ireland, for its people, for society?

How can we understand conflict better in order to build positive relations, improve communication, and nurture a society still limping from a severe disruption colloquially called the Troubles?

Over 50 years ago, Ray Davey radically declared that 'if we Christians cannot speak the message of reconciliation, we have nothing to say', meaning that reconciliation is at the heart of life and living for those who call themselves Christian and for all those of good will who want a better world for *all* people.

My hope is that these stories re-voice and reframe the work of reconciliation, using Corrymeela as a particular lens. They are stories about people trying (and regularly failing) to 'live' reconciliation, and they are stories about how to 'be' reconciliation wherever we find (or lose) ourselves: for parents struggling to be parents, for children lost for attention, for the dying, for the angry, for teachers, accountants, builders, cooks and cleaners, for politicians, clergy, bankers, artists.

Almost 10,000 people a year come to Corrymeela for rest, for challenge, for training, for encounter, for education. This is a small collection of stories from such events, mostly from my time as Centre Director (2009–14). Over its long history, Corrymeela has been involved in many private, confidential meetings. Enemies close but in separate rooms. Enemies far away in the same room. Families falling apart. Different faiths trying to get past the binary of 'us and them'. People from across the world and around the corner.

Most of those stories are not included. For two reasons: to respect the confidentiality of process, and in an attempt to avoid the 'hero on the white horse'.

So, a sack of tales.

Sad, funny, tragic, alien, true.

The title of this book derives from the rhythm of Corrymeela. Twice a day – morning and evening – a large bell sounds out over the six-acre site overlooking Rathlin Island. This is a call to pause, a call to come to the Croí, and to worship and reflect on God, self, neighbour, stranger. A bell also rings out at every mealtime, asking all present to pause and take a moment of thanks for the food. So, the centre is bounded by bells – morning, evening, mealtimes. And all of our life together is what we do between the bells.

SOUNDINGS

Thanks

Today the dining room in the main house at Corrymeela is full of people talking and eating. People from many countries. Mostly speaking in English. Two Germans have found each other and are telling jokes fluidly in their mother tongue. A wonderful German volunteer once said to me: 'Paul, you know, I am very funny in German.' I did not speak German. He was not funny in English. But I could hear his frustration. He was funny in another world.

Today at the tables are hungry mouths from the Philippines, Germany, the USA, Hungary, Ireland, England and Ghana. The queue at the kitchen hatch has dribbled to a stop. The staff and volunteers who have prepared the meal can take the weight off their Crocs for a well-earned half hour. A volunteer stands up, picks up a palm-sized metal Tibetan singing bowl and a small carved wooden stick. Those new to the centre ignore the person standing until a high bell-drone enters the room – the Tibetan bowl rings out over the assembled, struck firmly by the little Tibetan drumstick. The regulars set down their sharp utensils and stop chewing. New visitors look up, wondering about the bell-noise. Other guests are caught up in food and conversation and ignore the resonance in the air. The person holding the bowl (known affectionately as the Dinger) welcomes people to the centre – new groups and individuals are named and particularly greeted.

Welcomes are important. The shy stay shy but note that someone has said they are welcome. They will wait and see if this is true *in their experience*. The loud stay loud, conditioned to believe that volume is authority in every situation. Then (working from a well-used script), the person with the Dinger says: 'We have a tradition here at Corrymeela, where we take a moment of silence to give thanks for the food in our own way. Let's do that now.' What people do in that moment is up to their own conscience. There is no 'police check' on the inner life at Corrymeela.

What I say at this time is *thank you, thank you, thank you*. And I am reminded (and I need to be reminded) of those who produced the food – in both fair and oppressive circumstances. And I feel unfairly blessed. I don't fear hunger today. I can eat when I like, unlike many across this broken-scale world. And I am reminded and give thanks for the men and women who made this food for us today. And I am reminded of the mystery of life behind each breath, and I am caught up in praise for God, the Breath within each breath. On good days. On bad days, I wait for the silence to end because I am hungry, and my food is getting cold. But we create this space for thanksgiving every time we eat.

A lot of visitors over the age of fifty find this ritual 'very quaint, very old-fashioned' and they are comforted by this anachronistic habit. Teenagers not brought up religious find it amusing, embarrassing, perplexing. 'What the f**k was that?' is a regular refrain. Those chafing with historical hurts from religious encounters resist the way the moment of silence is framed: *It sounds religious. Religion hurt me. Therefore, I will resist this silence. I will resist this thanksgiving because there is no one in the silence to give thanks to.* They are not able to listen to what has been said: 'We take a moment of silence to give thanks for the food in our own way.' We want to give thanks for the food. This is a primal thing, a human thing. We are alive because of this food. We are alive because of the earth that we are eating. We are connected to many people – those who grew, picked, cleaned, packed. This is more than symbolic. This is actually what is keeping us alive! But it's a moment, and no one is (or should ever be) forced to have an epiphany. In fact, history has shown that being forced to love is not love. Power and love. Love and God. Love and neighbour. It's all here in this moment of silence: what we do between the bells. And we emphasize the phrase *in our own way* in order to allow the greatest breadth of opening for thanksgiving. I love these moments. They nudge me aware.

Many people 'step up' to the role of ringing the Dinger. Some are naturally gifted and command the room. Others are painfully coy about trying to stop 60 people from eating by whacking a Tibetan bowl with a twig. And regularly the wooden stick for the bowl is 'lost or mislaid', and spoons and knives take its place. It doesn't sound as good, but I'd rather hear a comedy *doink* than nothing at all. We create a platform for volunteers and staff to practise, giving affirmation for what they intended as much as for what they achieved. And so, we get the script variations of the nervous novice and the tongue-tied traveller, mumble-stumbling over a painful sentence: 'Let's shut up our eyes and give thank You, Now.' Or: 'Hello, everybody, let's pray for thanks. Inside I mean. Quietly. I mean, into yourself. OK?'

The words don't always make sense. They don't always need to. Sometimes it's a second-language confusion. Sometimes it's a shy-in-the-spotlight stutter. I have grace for any person who gives it a go. Sometimes tension reduces the silence to a millisecond, the quicker to finish and escape the burning limelight. Sometimes the silence is so long that people start to shuffle with the strangeness of a shared silence. Every day at every meal, someone stands and dares to ask us to stop and give thanks. It's a beautiful and un-pious tradition: 'Look. I'm standing before you, unarmed, holding a Tibetan singing bowl and (hopefully) an appropriate wooden stick. I'm going to pause and give thanks now. What are you going to do?'

Primary school groups are amazing to watch as they navigate this new rhythm to mealtimes, especially if they are around for a few days. First meals with kids are loud and bruising affairs if the teacher does not step in with a strategic 'Shush, children!' Many volunteers have lost their nerve after surrendering the stage to young children being excited, away from home and eating chips with tomato ketchup. But even by the second meal there is a difference. The kids know the silence is coming, and that it's not coming to get them. They are still excited, but also less nervous. So, the noise levels reduce. By the third meal they are getting the idea and quiet down for the moment of silence. A few of the boys snigger when they see each other's faces trying to be sober and still – it's not a sight they often encounter. It's a confusing sight. There is a concentration for a difficult maths question. But there is something to be solved in that. Here, in this moment, there is a silence and the odd request to *give thanks*. What on earth for? There is a concentration for a PlayStation game, but again there is a task, often involving being someone else killing other people. But *this* is a silence with seemingly nothing in it for them. No reward. After one particularly long moment of silence, a fantastic youth worker knew me enough to say this: 'So, Paul, do you think a wee prayer to God will make it all better? You don't know my kids!' I felt my defences rise and so I said nothing. It was good to have her here.

This is the problem with rituals. If they are empty for you, they are empty, no matter how meaningful they are for others. An international visitor once said to me: 'Paul, I have a respect for your symbols and rituals, but they mean nothing to me. Nothing.'

She wasn't being rude. She wasn't trying to be offensive or provocative. She knew how much these things meant to me. But they were empty vessels for her. How do we encourage and stay in these conversations? She continued: 'This is my third time here at Corrymeela. The first time I thought you were trying to convert me, and all I could hear were my parents' voices saying: "Religion is a nonsense." But I love this place, and I see what it has done for other people. And I see what it has done for me, how I have changed. And my parents have seen this change. But I can't tell them that Corrymeela is religious. I'm convinced about Corrymeela, but not by its symbols.'

After the moment of silence, there is a request for people to help with the dishes. And then the day clinks on, with perhaps the awareness that in pausing for a collective silence, a compass point might have been found for the next part of the journey.

Mobile

Artist Jonny McEwen loves his gadgets. He is one of my closest friends. He has a head for abstract painting, mathematics, creative community building and technology. He has been involved with Corrymeela for many years, starting when he returned to Ireland after living in Germany, where he was an eco-activist.

After his time as a volunteer, Jonny recognized that he could not get up to the centre at Ballycastle quite as often. He wondered how he might keep a connection/solidarity to the rhythm of a place he did not physically inhabit. He came up with a simple idea. He set his phone alarm to *beep!* at 9 pm, the same time that the bells would be ringing out at the centre for evening worship and reflection. He did not set his phone alarm to go off at 9.30 am. He was a realist. And not a morning person. So, wherever he was, whatever he was doing, his technology could remind him of community. That when his phone went *beep!* a bell was ringing on a hill overlooking the sea, and that Corrymeela was readying itself for yet another time of worship and reflection. He knew that not all of the worship times would be competent. He knew that some of them would really annoy him if he was actually there. He knew that some of the worship would be poorly attended, sometimes only having the person who had prepared the worship (a humbling experience). But he allowed himself to be *beeped!* into attention. Sometimes for a few seconds, sometimes longer. He remembers he is connected. He was connected before the beep from his phone, but now he is awake to this connection. When he told me about his daily alarms I was strangely moved.

At 9 pm every night a phone is going *beep!* This is both a burden and a possibility.

A burden in that it can feel like there is no escape from being responsible. And the possibility of being moved out of spiritual slumber.

Behold, I stand at the door and beep.

Broken

I have always been aware of who came before me at Corrymeela. Daunted and inspired to consider who has been in my role over the past 45 years. Ronnie Miller was the Centre Director who had handed me the reins, the keys, the weight. (He now lives in Boston doing amazing work with the Irish Immigration Centre.) Ronnie remained in touch and occasionally I would email or phone to ask about delicate matters or meetings/events he had attended. Ronnie had great project management skills, and had delighted in the rebuilding of the volunteer house (Coventry). He had also been involved in the early planning stages of developing the site (which would eventually lead to the demolition of two old buildings and the construction of a new residential space – the Davey Village). On a visit to the centre before the new building was completed, Ronnie gave me a gift. Or rather, he gave Corrymeela a gift – a large (12-inch diameter) ornate, hefty metal Tibetan singing bowl. Complete with its own beautifully carved stick, to make the bowl sing. He said: 'This is for the new building. It would mean a lot to me if you could use it to usher in the moments of silence to the new place.' I tried out the bowl in his presence. It rang out loud and clear. I was delighted with it.

When the new building was eventually open for visitors, one of the first groups to stay there was an energetic youth group from Northern Ireland. On day one, a dripping, abstract-art, tea-stain appeared on a newly painted white wall in the dining room. On day two, hot chocolate stains adorned the new cushions, and permanent marker had been used on the whiteboard. 'Somebody loves somebody', it said on the whiteboard. Accompanied by a heart drawing. In permanent marker. 'Somebody loves somebody.' Good to know.

At each mealtime the Tibetan bowl had been well-inducted into the community. I walked around the building when the group had departed, reviewing how it had stood up to its first acts of hospitality. I noted the tea-stains and the marks on the cushions and the permanent confession of love on the whiteboard. The group had enjoyed being at Corrymeela. They had learnt a lot, most of which they could not get down on an evaluation page. I picked up the Tibetan bowl and its stick and decided to let it ring out in a drone of aural thanks. I hit the bowl with the stick. No ringing. More a tinny *thitt* sound. Maybe I had not hit it properly. I tried again. No ringing out. I looked carefully at the beautiful, ornate gift. It was cracked. It takes a lot of force to crack a heavy Tibetan bowl. Hospitality costs. My rosy post-residential glow was dying. The cost of welcoming was being calculated. Beautiful bowls break. I wondered what I would tell Ronnie: Your lovely gift is broken. We don't use it any more. Kids wrecked it. I'm sorry.

It took me six months to write and tell him. He understood. Beautiful bowls break. Gifts are given with hope and expectation. And no guarantees.

When?

Question: When is a Tibetan singing bowl the wrong tool to use with a group?

When it's a particular clan of conservative Christians on a residential, who believe that every time I hit the bowl a devil enters the room, because that is the sound of a devil, because that is a bowl from Tibet, where the bowl is used by Buddhists, who are not Christian and so cannot be listened to and must be rejected.

(I stopped doing it after the leader of the group took me aside at tea-break and explained everything and then prayed for me.)

When it's a group of hard-nosed, fast-working business leaders who are at the centre for a training day, and who don't want any reference outside of their own economic paradigm. The Tibetan-bowl sound is for them the sound of pension-free activists, hippies, do-gooders, lefties, pie-in-the-sky arty types. This sound is not of the real world, their real spread-sheet, finance-driven, target-laden world.

(I kept it up the whole day, acutely aware of how they felt. Offering a different world.)

When it's drawing a line with the last straw. When it is the last in a series of ambient sounds that the international expert in restorative justice has introduced to a group of very experienced community activists from the island of Ireland. When the group have already endured nose-flute music from worthy orphans who learnt to play these terrible instruments and, in so doing, have turned their lives around. When the group have already endured Native American chanting and the waving of an eagle feather by a white man in his sixties.

The bowl was a hell's bell and it was now getting in the way of learning. At one of the tea-breaks a droll therapist discreetly whispered in my ear: 'What's next for our musical delight? The f**king Beatles played on the panpipes?'

(I spoke to the expert about the cultural dissonance being created by his musical choices. He held on to his eagle feather. And lost the group.)

Seven contracts

01.

At that point, his phone rings.

At the *almost-there* in the thick of a mediation, where a new map is offered of a way forward that guarantees pain, but less pain than before, acknowledging the cuts and the limits of trust, where the strain to keep the parties in the room is minutely measured against the tension that might break the truce into words of fury and flashes of fist.

At that point, his phone rings. One of the parties in the dispute.

He looks at me. He looks to the other party (in the dispute) who was in full-flow costly-honest commentary.

The phone keeps ringing.

I say: 'Remember the mediation contract?'

And he says: 'Yes. I remember. Phones off. I've got to take this.'

He quickly leaves the room, whispering, 'What?' into his answered phone.

'What did I tell you?' says the other party in the room. 'He does not respect the process. He does not respect me.'

'Maybe it's an emergency,' I say. 'He has young kids.'

'I have young kids!' shouts the phone-free other party. 'I have emergencies!! This just confirms to me that he is not interested in a deal.'

I begin to imagine how I can repair the damaged thread of trust caused by the ringing of a phone.

~

02.

I am instructed to remove my shoes. This is a former police station. A black cat walks across the wooden floor. This is a Buddhist temple in London. Everywhere there are pictures of the Dalai Lama smiling. There are 'real' Tibetan singing bowls for sale. I brought my own. I am here to train a group of international mediators. We stare at our shoeless feet. We begin with introductions and a learning contract – how we are to learn in this space. A blunt broad-shouldered Russian (ex-military) smiles and says: 'I do not do contracts.' Half the room nod in agreement. A quarter look concerned. The rest are unreadable. He says: 'When people come to us they are anxious, angry. No one is listening in the beginning.'

I say: 'How do you deal with inappropriate behaviour in a mediation?'

He says: 'We mention it when it happens. Then we stop it! No one is listening in the beginning.'

I continue talking, continue creating a contract for learning. It is the beginning of the day. I am not sure who is listening. The Russian is smiling.

~

03.

All visitors to Corrymeela receive a speech, which is equal parts welcome, health and safety, info about the site, and invitation to the rhythm of the community. Regarding smoke and fire alarms, people are told what to do if an alarm goes off and where to gather. People are told to leave their belongings and exit the building. And not to go back into the building until the 'all-clear' is given.

During one memorable fire alarm, a youth group from England, coming to learn about dealing with conflict, were jolted out of their afternoon slumber to gather outside the Davey Village. Volunteers then proceeded to run through the building, primarily to get everyone out, and then to seek out the source of the alarm. They knock on doors and carry out head-counts. On this particular alarm, the numbers did not tally. One person was missing. Bed-plans were consulted. Their bedroom door was located. Their bedroom door was rapped. Their bedroom door was hammered. Their bedroom door was shouted at. Their bedroom door remained closed, locked from the inside. After a fraught few minutes, the source of the alarm was detected: in one room (not the locked one), the heavy smell of anti-perspirant spray – a tell-tale clue that a person or persons had been overly vigorous with under-arm spray, had missed their armpits and sprayed upwards to the smoke detectors in the ceiling. Spray. Spray. Alarm. The cover speech talks explicitly about this. *Spray downward. The sensors are sensitive.* No one is listening in the beginning.

The mystery and frustration of the missing person was later revealed. The young man came out of his room with dripping wet hair, shorts and a t-shirt. 'I heard the alarm,' he said. 'But I would have been safe, because I was in the shower, and fires can't get into the shower.' One of the youth leaders despairingly shook his head and grabbed the youth for a one-on-one session on fire alarms and smoke inhalation.

~

04.

An anxious teenage boy turns quickly to the sound of the 9 pm call to the Croí.

'What's that, a church bell?'

It was his first time here. I explain about the Corrymeela rhythm and what the bell signified, feeling suitably happy with my explanation.

'Tell me this,' he says. 'Is it a Protestant or a Catholic bell?'

We had a lot to talk about.

~

05.

Sometimes bets were placed, often by volunteers gifted at holding the silence in a room at mealtimes. The bet was this: Ring the bell at a mealtime. Ask for a moment's silence. Then, see how long you can keep the silence. The knack, apparently, was to avoid eye-contact, especially with the other volunteers or the Centre Director.

What happens when you stretch a practice that is institutionally 'serious and meaningful'? Could a joke stretch a ritual so far that it breaks? That's some powerful humour. Reminds me of going as a furious teenager to a Friday night youth club in a Methodist Church Hall. I was attracted by the warmth, football, and an audience of females. At the end of each evening, the true purpose of the central heating and the tuck shop and the football became clear: The Epilogue – a time to share something about Jesus being THE Saviour. My friends and I were not church-goers, were not interested in 'being saved'. Not if it meant giving up on what made us teenagers, which was not thinking about the future, swearing, alcohol, 'getting off with someone', and fixating over music that adults couldn't/shouldn't/mustn't like. But we had enough sense to know that this was the contract – you got football in exchange for a five-minute preach at the end of the night. We sat impatiently during the sermon, but started to get agitated if the closing prayer stretched out for too long. One night the overly zealous youth leader got carried away with his prayers for starving children in Africa and stretched 'the serious bit' too far, and as he reached yet another peak of sincerity and intercession I let rip with a fart that shook the room with shock and laughter. It got me banned for a month. And stopped the intercessional prayer. But come on, you can't stretch 'the serious' that far, in that context, and not risk the whole thing collapsing, winded.

Back to the bet: *Let's take a moment of silence to give thanks for the food.* How long is the moment today? And how to fill the moment with meaning? Or how to find the meaning waiting in the moment? And how to live with the risk of a precious ritual being refused/abused in a multi-storied world.

~

06.

It is 2012, and many weapons have been decommissioned in Ireland. From all sides: hand-guns, rocket launchers, explosives, machine-guns, sniper-rifles, ammunition. The first Corrymeela Centre Director, Harold Goode, was one of the official 'witnesses', verifying that the weapons had been 'put beyond use'. And the British Army have mostly departed. And the police service has been re-named and differently recruited. And there is power-sharing between political enemies. And today I am hosting a silent retreat for 15 people. A day of introducing people to what is already there – silence. And to what is waiting in the silence.

The day begins in the Croí with gentle music, a lit candle, a welcome, and a contract. One aspect of the contract is proving difficult for some participants. I have asked everyone to 'hand over' their phones – to turn the technology off and to symbolically set it down, on the round table that also holds a lit candle, a turf cross and an open Bible. I laugh and call it a de-commissioning. Most laugh. Most press the off-button on their phones and hand them over. One person asks if she can take it back at lunch-time. (Agreed.) Another asks if she can take her phone back at break times (there will be two) *and* lunch. We discuss this and I suggest it may get in the way of the process. She reluctantly agrees to let go of her phone. One person holds his phone and looks at the candle. He is a member of the clergy. He is a warm, generous, thoughtful, hospitable human. But he is struggling to turn off his phone and hand it over to me. He throws out a few sentences: someone may have an emergency; someone may have died; someone may need my assistance. I let the sentences sit. I was not going to force a contract on anyone. I can look at lunch-time? (I nod.) When is lunch-time? (Three hours.)

He places his temporarily decommissioned phone on to the table, nudging the candle, which flickers brighter for a few seconds. Contract agreed, we continue. Into silence. Into 'ways of being' in the silence.

At lunch-time we eat together, also in silence. Giving feedback on this new eating experience, one of the participants spoke of how strange yet liberating it had been to eat without speaking: no pressure to be funny, clever, profound or relevant. How much said in so few words.

During the final sharing about the day (not in silence), the reluctant decommissioner sat balancing his phone in the open palm of his right hand. After thanking me for the day, he paused, then said: 'I've been thinking about my phone all day. I've been thinking about why I struggled to give it up. And my conclusion is this: I wanted to be phoned. I wanted to be ... needed.' And then his voice trailed off.

How much said in so few words. What the silence reveals.

~

07.

Twice a day a bell sounds over Corrymeela. Everyone on site is made aware of what this signifies. It is a time to pause. A time to recall the heart. A call to the heart. People are invited to the Croí, to sit and be present with themselves, with friends, staff, strangers, and to consider the Divine Other in their midst.

Morning and evening the bell rings. It is a planned event, led by staff, volunteers and community members. Sometimes a liturgy is followed, plucked from the well-thumbed Corrymeela worship book. At other times the Croí becomes a place where kids laugh and jump at a story told using puppets. The ringing of the bells is a call to wonder, a call to wait, a place to practise being present.

Three symbols are on the small wooden table. Candle, Bible, Celtic cross. Twice a day the candle is lit and extinguished. Hope stirs as the candle is danced by the wind. Between light and darkness something happens. The Bible is opened, sometimes randomly, sometimes with intention. Give us this day our holy words ... The Celtic cross squats black and quiet – a Roman instrument for slow execution, transformed into a memory of death transformed by love. And there is no magic formula in the placing of these objects together. And there is no power source turned on and off by the lighting and snuffing of a candle. But there is possibility. An invitation to ponder, to dream, to be renewed. To encounter a presence in the midst of feeling forsaken. A place for pilgrims – a levelling place for doubters, believers, stumblers and searchers. A place to embrace our particular oddness and strangeness. And when the bell rings, no one knows what will happen next. Who will attend? Who will host? What will be uttered or stuttered in a shy faint voice? What might be renewed in repetition?

And it is a wonder to be here.

Twice a day the bell sounds over Corrymeela. Except when there is a youth or children's group on site. In which case the bell is whacked and gonged and tolled and pealed all the long day long:

'Look, Mummy, a bell!'
'Can I ring it?'
'Can I ring it again?'
('Can I ring it too?')
'No, it's still my turn!'
('I can do it louder than you!')
'No, you can't!'
('Mummy, he hit me!')
'No, I didn't.'
'I found the bell first!'
('I saw it first.')
'I don't want to share the bell.'
('I hate you!')
'I hate you!!'

Again and again and again the bell sounds out, declaring the clang of children on site, exploring. And in those dissonant moments I occasionally contemplate borrowing a chain-saw and cutting down the wooden bell-tower, and throwing the bell into the sea.

For the fish to quietly ring with curious tails.

GROUNDINGS

One.

I see Ray everywhere.

Towering over Mother Teresa. Sitting attentive with students. Formal and upright, welcoming a prince. Holding hands with the Dalai Lama. Playing full-back for the Ulster Rugby squad. Nodding approval with former Centre Directors. Leaning in to politicians – listening, engaged. Looking out to sea with famous academics. In the pulpit, calling on the angels. With Kathleen, his wife, arm-in-arm. His images and memory are all around the centre. And I spoke his prayers long before I had ever been to Corrymeela. Throughout the nineties I recited this prayer:

> In the midst of hunger and war
> We celebrate the promise of plenty and peace.
> In the midst of oppression and tyranny
> We celebrate the promise of service and freedom.
> In the midst of doubt and despair
> We celebrate the promise of faith and hope.
> In the midst of fear and betrayal
> We celebrate the promise of joy and loyalty.
> In the midst of hatred and death
> We celebrate the promise of love and life.
> In the midst of sin and decay
> We celebrate the promise of salvation and renewal.
> In the midst of the dying Lord
> We celebrate the promise of the living Christ.[1]

A prayer that faces the world in all its pain, hate and fear, but that also sees something else/someone else 'in the midst' of life in all its torn and beautiful tapestry. Hope is not about being in denial.

In the early days of taking up the post of Centre Director, I was anxious to read all the 'sacred scrolls', to be inspired and kept on the right path(s). On one particularly fretful day when I must have been manifesting my anxiety about following the founders, one community member said, in almost a scold: 'This is your time. This is your time to make it up. I will support you.' Which was very encouraging. Which was true. Until I did something like move a falling-apart painting that had been made in a very special session by someone very important. Then it was not true. Then it was: 'You don't know. You don't know the importance of that painting. It's precious! I was there. You weren't there. You don't know.' At times, it seemed like every blade of grass had a story that needed to be divined and commemorated. I had to tread gently. I had to honour and learn from the ancestors. And I was regularly told: 'This is your time. This is your time to make it up. I will support you.' Discernment was required, as I searched for the Spirit in the midst of hectic schedules, hordes of people, and broken cups once held by someone important.

Ray was the founder of Corrymeela. He was fifty-five years old when the community formally began in 1965. Denounced, so the story goes, by the Free Presbyterian Church and its leader, the Reverend Ian Paisley, who called us diabolical for being ecumenical. Imagine! Bringing Protestants and Catholics together to talk about peace, reconciliation, God and neighbourliness! Outrageous in 1965. And then the Troubles began in 1968, and this outrageous idea became something to die for – Protestants and Catholics coming together, sometimes at great cost. Having to return to their suspicious communities to answer the questions: Where have you been? Who were you with?

And Corrymeela and Ray became famous. Famous for creating safe spaces to rest, to engage, to question, to have difficult conversations. When I tell the Corrymeela origin story I begin in Germany. Germany during World War Two, where Ray is a prisoner of war. In his *War Diaries* he writes: 'Washing conditions were unimaginable and exercise in the very confined space was incredibly difficult. Food was another huge problem and we were never satisfied.'[2] Corrymeela: formed from hunger, dissatisfaction, prison and war. And something else 'in the midst'. I try to encourage listeners to this origin story to imagine what these prisoner-of-war conditions might do to a person's head. What questions might be circling mercilessly in the mind? What rage might be pulsing through the veins? What prayer might be shaped in a row of empty-bellied nights feeling abandoned by God? In my telling of the origin story, I take listeners to Dresden – a beautiful German city. I take listeners to this beautiful city on 13 February 1945. This beautiful city that had so far escaped being bombed by the Allies. This beautiful city that had once housed one of the greatest art collections in the world. This beautiful city full of refugees, fleeing the Russian Advance. This beautiful city with disputed military importance. And I say: 'This is where Corrymeela was formed.'

Ray was a prisoner-of-war in a camp 15 miles from Dresden. Ray saw Dresden before and after the Allies. Before and after the bombing of Dresden by the Allies. By *his* team. By *his* side. And as I recount the origins of Corrymeela in those bloody seconds, I give out statistics: 13 February 1945: An evening raid by the RAF, Codename Thunderclap; 800 aircraft; 650,000 incendiaries;

80,000lb of high explosives; two waves of attack. Virtu-
ally no anti-aircraft fire from the ground.

In my telling of the Corrymeela origin story I give voice
to some who witnessed the attack on Dresden: 'As soon
as one part of Dresden was on fire, the bombers moved
on to another part of the city, until the whole place was
ablaze. The fires were visible for hundreds of miles.'

Ray saw the chaos from his camp. What might people
have prayed during those moments? What might the
Allies' Chaplain have uttered just before the men took
to their planes? Safe home. Aim true. Get the bastards.
Lord, protect them. (Who? The pilots? The civilians?)
And what might the German priest have prayed as he
heard the sirens that told him that enemy planes were
coming? Lord, protect us! Save us. British Bastards. Miss.

And in my telling of the Corrymeela origin story I
show photographs of the city after the bombing (which
was continued the next afternoon by the Americans, and
then the day after by the British again). Buildings melted.
Roads cracked. Cars exploded. Homes destroyed. Bodies
burnt and shrivelled. A city ruined. Ray visited Dresden
a short while after the bombing, on 12 March 1945. I
invite people to imagine a city in chaos. I ask: 'What type
of questions might be coming up for Ray? If the Allies
did this, who are the "good guys"? What type of God
would allow this to happen? What type of person can
see this and believe in a loving God? What does it mean
to love your enemy when your ally does this?' And then
I get Ray to speak, and I quote from his *War Diaries*: 'It
looked as if some super-natural giant had taken up the
town and shaken it and then set it on fire. I walked for a
very long time without seeing a house fit for habitation. I
had never seen such absolute devastation on such a wide
scale.'[3]

Some super-natural giant.

And because the city was so full of unrecorded refugees, exact numbers of those killed vary. The estimates range from 25,000 to 100,000. Men, women, children. Set on fire by the 'good guys'. Set alight by their righteousness. Hit by bomb crews doing their jobs, commanded by their superiors. This is the beginning of Corrymeela, I say. Not the Troubles in Northern Ireland. In the midst of death, the promise of life. Not in some hereafter heaven. But the kingdom of God on earth. In the midst. What kind of God can be present in the midst of such fiery, brutal horror? After Dresden, many could not imagine such a God, and lost their faith in something divine.

I once told this origin story to a group of students from Bradford University. They were Peace Studies Undergraduates. There were two Germans in the class.

After telling this Dresden story, one of the Germans raised his hand and said:

'My grandmother …'
Then he paused.
And then he said: 'My grandmother was there. Dresden. She was there. She never …'
And then he trailed off …
'She never spoke about it.
It's hard to talk about this stuff in Germany.
The "Far Right" have colonized this conversation.
And so, you are accused of being Fascist if you want to talk about it. You can't talk about it.
My grandmother was there.
She never …'

I try to direct the Corrymeela origin story to both head and heart, and try to explore connections with those who visit, who bring their own conflict stories. Some have so much agony and grief that they are unable to find hope, believing that hope is a betrayal of the dead and that recovery is a denial of history. Some find brief relief. Some find a lifelong vocation.

~

One lunch-time, Pauline came and sat down at my table. Pauline is a nurse, mother, wife, Catholic, community member. We ate together, traded small talk until we had finished our food. I sensed Pauline had something more than 'pass the salt' to say to me.

'Can I say something to you?' This did not sound like more small talk about the weather. 'Please,' I said, hoping it was not a criticism warming up. She said: 'You need to go and see Ray. It's important.' Ray was now ninety-six, frail, living with his daughter. I had been Centre Director for 18 months and I had not yet visited Ray. In fact, although I talked about Ray a lot, I had never met Ray in person. I was slightly embarrassed by this fact. Pauline looked at me directly and said it again: 'You need to go and see Ray. It's important.' I agreed. We set a provisional date, time and place to meet, to be confirmed by Alison, Ray's daughter (and now primary caregiver).

And so, on the appointed day, I am driving to meet Ray for the first time. And as I drive to meet one of my heroes, I start to plan what to say, how to behave. I am nervous. It is said that we should never meet our heroes. Ray is ninety-six, fragile, living with his daughter. What sort of shape will he be in? Will he give me his blessing – anoint me to carry on his work? I want the encounter to be heroic, special, epic. I fear I may disappoint Ray, and dearly hope he will be impressed.

And then I arrive, pull up outside a house I have never been to before, to meet Ray Davey, founder of Corrymeela – ninety-six years old, frail, living with his daughter Alison, who greets us at the front door. I had been following Pauline's car, and she steps out and embraces Alison. They know each other. I shake her hand, formally. How does it feel, I wonder, to have a series of serious strangers come to meet your father? Do you ever want to say: 'He's flesh and blood, urine and sweat, saliva and spills, tripping and shaking, familiar, a stranger?' Do you ever want to prick the saintly bubble and say: 'He was a terrible cook and a distant dad?' Alison does not say this today. Today she says, 'Welcome', and invites us into her warm house. She gives us a well-worn run-down of instructions: 'Dad's in here. He's not great. Just talk to him and hold his hand.'

I am guided into a long living room. At the far end of the room is an old man slumped in a comfy armchair: grey-haired, sunken-cheeked, freshly shaven, head fallen, eyes closed. Ray. Pauline guides me over to Ray. She bends down and says a firm 'Hello' into his face, kisses his cheek. Ray stirs, opens his eyes and smiles. To Ray she says, 'This is Paul, the new Centre Director. He's here to see you.' And to me she says: 'Sit down beside him.' I do.

Pauline and Alison take seats at the far end of the room and start to chat. About children, the weather, health, haircuts. I am to have an audience when I meet Ray. Or is it a judging panel? Hold his hand and talk to him were the instructions. My hands are sweating. I can't shake his hand with a slippery paw! I want to make the right impression. I have worn my smart-casual outfit: heavy brown corduroy trousers (not ideal for a sauna-temperature environment); crème shirt (moistening rapidly under the armpits); green tie (from Oxfam); brown wool jacket, expensive (also from Oxfam), minus one button (lost). A pair of shorts, flip-flops, and a t-shirt would have been more practical, but I find it hard to have any sense of decorum wearing flip-flips.

I wipe my right hand quickly on my corduroy trousers and shake Ray's hand and say, 'Hello.' Ray opens his eyes and looks at me. 'Your face is very sweaty' is what I half-expect him to say, but he says nothing. He keeps a hold of my hand. First contact has been made. And now I am stuck. Because Ray has fallen asleep holding my hand. And I don't know what to do next. 'Show him pictures of the new volunteers,' shouts Pauline from the other end of the room. I release myself from Ray's grip and take out A4 photocopied images of the long-term volunteers. Ray looks asleep. Do I waken him? Can he understand anything I am saying? I have come here expecting something epic, for Ray to open his mouth and proclaim profundities. Words that I can treasure for ever. Wisdom that I can tell others about. Ray looks asleep. I am here for that special mountain-top experience. This is Ray Davey. One of my heroes. The founder of the centre where I am now Director. I tell his story every week to strangers. *Ray, tell me a story. Tell me a story I will never forget. Tell me a secret that's just between us. Tell me. Help me. Set me right.* Ray looks asleep. I look at Alison who nods and smiles. She has seen this scenario many times. A person coming face-to-face with the shell of her father. Does she think, *I held this man's hand for safety on the first day of school?* Or does she think, *He never held my hand. He was not a great hugger of the family. Only strangers.*

I don't know. I love to hold my children's hands. It brings me a primitive joy. I hope my children will say in later years, 'My dad was great crack – he held my hand, told great stories at bedtime, took us hunting for conkers, pushed us out into the waiting roaring sea.'

But my fear is that they will say, 'My father spent our childhood trying to save the world. He was great when he was at home. He wasn't at home much.' This is my fear – that I have 'saved' strangers and lost my own children. I bring the first image up to his face and say: 'Ray, these are the new volunteers. Ray?' He opens his eyes and reaches almost instinctively for the A4 splash of colour. 'Ray – this is Roland, from the Philippines – he makes the world a more beautiful place.' Ray holds the photo of Roland. Ray shakes Roland in his trembling hand, then drops him on the carpeted floor. Roland smiles from the floor. I leave Roland and continue. I say: 'This is Valentine. Valentine is from Germany. He is eighteen years old. His English is fantastic and getting even better. He likes to go off site with a bike and a tent.'

Ray has grasped the picture of Valentine. Did he come alive when I said the word 'Germany'? I know Ray has a strong connection to Germany. Is Ray remembering bodies burnt by firebombs in the name of truth? Ray holds on to Valentine, then lets this particular image of a German go. Valentine joins Roland on the ground.

I say: 'This is Jeni. From Northern Ireland. A grafter. Funny. Sassy. Amazing cook. A clergyman's daughter.' Ray stares at Jeni. He is a former clergyman. He has a daughter. Ray hands Jeni back to me. I say: 'This is Saraswati from Hungary – she is a linguist, loves film, has introduced me to an amazing film – *As It Is in Heaven* – a Swedish morality tale. I think I am saying her name wrong. She says it doesn't matter. She says she is used to it. Used to being mistakenly named. Misnamed.'

I am starting to get into a rhythm with Ray. Giving out some of my best lines. Ray is asleep again. Do I keep going? Keep talking to a slumped head? I keep going. I say: 'This is Yael, from the USA. New York. From the Jewish Tradition. She has lots to say most days about being the only Jew at Corrymeela. Yael is great with kids and youth groups – the right amount of energy and boundaries.' Ray is looking at the picture of Yael. His head is in the right direction and his eyes are open. I will take this as 'looking'. I am trying not to take this personally, that one of my heroes is not listening to me. The neurotic part of me thinks: *This is what he would have done in his prime – look at me like I am an idiot.* The more reasoned part of me thinks: *This man doesn't listen to very much of anything these days.* And the hopeful part of me imagines that something is happening between us, connections being made, in a way I cannot currently comprehend.

In the background, Alison and Pauline are chatting about holidays and possibly nursing. Or possibly nursing holidays. I continue. I say: 'Ray, this is Kat. From England. We have been doing a school project together on diversity. She has a degree in Peace Studies from Bradford. She is getting married soon.'

'And this is Frank. Frank is from Cameroon. He is quiet, loves football, Facebook, food. I am not sure how much he understands. I speak to him in faith that something is going in, that there is some comprehension. It must be tiring to be translating every day. And we speak our English so strangely here!' Ray drops Frank. I now know that there is no chance of being anointed *the special one* by Ray. I will politely get through this encounter, and chalk it up to another disappointing meeting with one of my heroes. I say to Alison: 'Is he getting tired?' hoping she would say yes, and I could stop. Alison smiles and says: 'No, he is fine. He may drift in and out. That's normal.' I continue.

There are two more volunteers to introduce. 'Ray, this is Andrew, also from the USA. A runner. Serious. Quiet. Thoughtful. Contemplating becoming a Minister. Athletic, religious – just like you, Ray!' Ray holds Andrew and stares. 'And finally, a local girl. This is Michaela. From Armagh. A maths graduate who loves books, chocolate, contemplation and playing the bodhran. What a combination!' Ray is awake and holding on to Michaela. What is it, Ray? What are you paying attention to? Ray doesn't answer. Instead he looks up at me (we are half a metre apart) and he looks at my face with a penetrating gaze. And then he says: 'You've got lovely eyes.' Well now, I wasn't expecting that. Ray Davey, the founder of Corrymeela, one of my heroes, has looked closely at my face and pronounced: 'You've got lovely eyes.'

I smile. Ray smiles. Our faces are close. He has my hand again. Ray is holding my hand and smiling into my face, having declared: 'You've got lovely eyes.' What to say next? What to do next? What to do with what Ray said? People know I am going to see Ray. They will say: 'What did he say to you?' And I will say: 'He said I had lovely eyes.' But before I can say even a thank you to Ray, his gaze glazes, his mind wanders, his head slumps and his eyes close. I was now feeling very awkward. I mean it's not such a great story, is it? It's not going to go into a history of Corrymeela, is it? The seventh Centre Director of Corrymeela was Paul Hutchinson. According to tradition, and we can't accurately say more than that, Ray Davey, in his ninety-sixth year, uttered to Paul that he had, and I quote, 'lovely eyes'. Many scholars have perused this line for its literal and metaphorical meanings.

Let's end the fantasy there. Jacob wrestled with an angel and was blessed with, among other things, a permanent limp and the knowledge that he was Beloved by God. I wrestled with the awkwardness of holding a ninety-six-year-old man's warm hand, in a sauna-hot living room, as he tells me that I have *lovely eyes*. Forgive me, Ray. I asked too much of you. You are frail, failing, and I wanted you to anoint me. Forgive me.

I had run out of photographs and anecdotes. I had met my expectations and I had been found wanting. Time to go. I stood up and indicated that it was time to exit.

Pauline and Alison stood. Pauline kissed and hugged Ray. Alison shook my hand. I thanked her. We left. It was a relief to be in the cold air, and out of the hothouse observation room.

I hugged Pauline and said, 'Thank you.' Pauline said, 'That was a good thing to do.'

I nodded and got in the car. We went our separate ways. On the drive back from Belfast to Ballycastle, I turn off the radio and begin to listen. Something was disturbing me about my meeting with Ray. I drive and listen. At the sign for Antrim – nothing. No insights. At the turn off for Ballymena – nothing. At the turn for Ballycastle – zero epiphanies. At the car park just past the golf course, with the view of the sea and Rathlin Island, a small notion nudges me. I pull over and stare at the sea. I check in on myself. I am physically tired. My eyes are sore, and my lower back is tight from hunching close to Ray. I am emotionally flat, feeling both that I have failed at something and that my hero had not lived up to expectations. Two failures.

And there it was, hiding behind the 'failures'. An itch in my soul. The small sign to take note of. There it was. A tiny wonder. I had been blind to the blessing. I had been gifted something and I had not understood. I mean, how often does anyone get to hold the hand of a ninety-six-year-old man, famous or obscure? The fact that Ray was a legend was not the blessing. It was this: that there is a blessing in holding the hand of a very old man. Not to think – *what has this hand put in motion?* Not to think of hands unveiling charred bodies with a shovel in the aftermath of Dresden. Not to think – *what famous hands has this hand shaken?* Not to think, but to experience

– the tremble, the warmth, the texture, the nails, the old scars, the feeble grip. To hold an old man's hand. Nothing more or less. I miss so much, thinking ahead or back. I miss the moments of living. I watch the sea and let it be.

Two.

I am greeted by an elegant early bird – a tall, dark-haired, handsome man, accustomed to turning up at events in a suit. He is the architect of the Davey Village. I had inherited his plans that, even at that early stage, had gone through many committees and iterations. I had been tasked with overseeing the demolition of the old 'village' and 'cottage' sections of Corrymeela, and with the construction of the new building, the Davey Village. And thanks to Shane O'Neill, my Centre Manager, I did not have to think about the detail. Shane was the weekly/daily/hourly contact point. Thank God! I was the person contacted when there were points to be clarified or in dispute. Many conversations had been logged to get to this point: the opening of the building.

There had been hate mail sent to me from people concerned and angry about the demolition of the old buildings, telling me I was wrong to knock down places that meant so much to so many people. I tried to keep discerning the important memories behind these criticisms. But some days it just felt like an attack. So I took the flak, held a candle-lit ritual to close the buildings, read from the book of Ecclesiastes, and gave the go-ahead for the bulldozers to begin pulling down buildings that were not fit for purpose. Poor heating, musty rooms, and temperamental fire alarms were not the future. Nostalgia and profound memories were not enough to keep the place safe, warm and habitable. Jarringly, one well-meaning community member had criticized me for including en suites in each of the rooms of the new Davey Village, the reasoning being that some of the people coming on residential would feel uncomfortable with such comforts. I was angry at this patronizing conversation, but hid my feelings, offering to feed back to the community member if anyone ever felt that the en suites were too 'posh'. No one has. But today, at the opening of the Davey Village, the architect is in high spirits.

This had been a big project for him, this early in his career, and he was justifiably proud. We joked about the journey to this moment, about potential design prizes, about cladding and landscape, and about how the building might impact on peace and reconciliation. It was all very light until he mentioned *that day*. The day that 'tools were downed'. The day the experts were called on-site for an emergency meeting. A 'collapse' had been reported in a field close to Corrymeela. Not being a builder or architect, I had not been clear about what 'a collapse in a field' actually was. It was not, thank God, a farmer hitting the dirt, holding his arm in agony. It was not the place where a wealthy landowner took the phone call that told him his stocks had devalued to pennies during the financial crisis. It was not (draw near) a young man angrily kicking clods of earth as he shed his family faith, his childhood beliefs, as he wondered what he could hold on to now in this new spinning world. No. In this particular case, 'a collapse' was a large hole unexpectedly appearing in the ground of a farmer's field. The farmer, on noticing this, had contacted the relevant authorities. And out of this, our building work had appeared on the radar of a special governmental gaze: The Abandoned Mines Committee.

And then we came to *that day*, where a gathering had been swiftly organized with the builders, site managers, architect, insurers and health and safety professionals. A roomful of people talking about foundations. A roomful of people reluctant to touch this issue, lest they be deemed responsible. A roomful of experts skirting around the issue in a maddening choreography, and the fear that the foundations of Corrymeela might not be adequate for the future, for this existing build. Building work had been carried out a few years ago with the development of the new volunteer house (Coventry). All the planning had been carried out 'by the book'. All relevant departments had been informed. But now here we were, with one person saying: 'We might need to stop the building work'. We were in the middle of the build, with the skeleton of the Davey Village rising higher every day. No one wanted to say anything *for sure*. No one wanted to say anything *for definite*. And those looking for a sermon in this meeting would have found a rich seam: Foundations. Buildings. Experts. Looking for a Judas to blame. The Pharisees playing it 'by the book'. And for a while I played the part of Peter, denying to myself over and over that this was happening, while reciting my crisis mantra: *Shit, Shit, Shit, Shit*. So, what happened next? A culprit found? A firing squad? A victim? A hanging of the head? A hanging? After much sweaty and legislative negotiation, a way forward was agreed by all the parties in the room. Building work would stop. Bore-holes would be drilled on the building site, to a depth of 40 metres, and a geologist would be on-site to take samples of each bore-hole at selected points in the drilling. This I could just about live with, even though it would delay completion of the building, and so reduce lettings income for the year. In this case, time was actually related to money, in a very particular and track-able way. No building, no rooms. No visitors, no income. The other recommendation was even more problematic: six bore-holes at random points across the whole site, to check for structural strength. The rest of the site was still active, and was coming into the summer programme, where literally hundreds of people of all ages would be on-site. I could see the future: little children curiously close to big machinery; daring teenagers peering down deep holes; wilful adults and 'Do Not Enter' signs; wheelchairs wobbling on cracked paths. I resisted this recommendation until I saw that there was no other option. However, I did manage to get one of the 'random' bore-hole sites moved from just outside the door of the main reception area. But in the end, we had a large ten-foot high drill surrounded by cones and 'No Entry' signs for most of that summer. Once drilling began, a geologist sat in her car reading a book until she was called to take a sample. I remember what she was reading – a book by Hilary Mantel. There would have been a poetic delight in telling you that the book in question was *Bring Up the Bodies*, but no, it was *Wolf Hall*. (Another well-reviewed book I have not (yet) read.) Curious, one day I asked the geologist a question, as she captured a sample of the black muck from underneath Corrymeela: 'How old is that stuff?' The geologist looked at me, looked at the black, and said: 'About 200 million years.' Then she walked away, as if I had merely asked the time of day, rather than the age of a black substance millions of years old. Geologist eyes: aware and awake to the long history of the world. For me this was an awful moment. As in, awe-inspiring. To suddenly become aware of what has always been underneath my feet. The ancient covered-history of the world. I was flooded with wonder and thanks. The miracle seen in the carboniferous muck. Should I remove my shoes to honour ancient creation? No. There were sharp rocks everywhere. Should I create a shrine to honour this dark matter? Yes, but not in the form of a plaque with words that reduce rather than explain this glorious creation. Yes, in the form of a new and sustained awareness, regard and protection of the planet. How might I now walk lightly on this place? The architect and I walk towards the tea and coffee being served at the opening of the new Davey Village. I mind my step.

Three.

Twelve months after the opening of the Davey Village, I am giving a tour of Corrymeela for two strangers who have appeared unannounced on-site. I am avoiding some paperwork, so I gladly agree to guide them around the site. We come to the Davey Village and I mention the darkness below and its age – 200 million years. 'According to the geologist,' says one of the strangers. 'Yes,' I said. 'The earth is not that age,' he says.

I smile and listen.

'According to the true Christian Tradition, the world was created only 6,000 years ago, by the Lord God Almighty.'

'According to whom?' I asked.

'According to God,' he said.

And then he asked me four quick-fire questions, wanting to know where I stood on these issues, so that he could know how to stand in relation to me. Was I for or against him?

'Is this really a Christian centre?'

'When were you washed in the blood of Jesus?'

'What church do you go to on Sunday?'

'Do you think the Bible is all true?' I have heard these questions so many times. I have been questioned so many times. By people trying to find the truth. This much I know: we are standing outside; the sun is warm on our faces; the dark waits underneath our feet, ancient, hidden; this is not the time or place to explore his questions. 'Let's continue the tour,' I say. 'This building is called the Croí, which is the Irish word for ...'

'Wait,' said the visitor. 'Let me stop you right there. Did you say it's an Irish word?'

Another trigger-word. There are trip-wires everywhere at this peace centre.

Ready to explode at the slip of a tongue, with the drop of an accent, with the glimpse of colour on a football top. This was going to be a long tour, with many colliding origin stories. I hope we can disagree well.

THE HEART TRANSLATED

What's in a word?

I speak at least one word of Irish every day. Not a common language where I grew up.

Not spoken in our house. Told that it was the language of the *enemy*. Told to be 'on guard' when I heard it spoken. But now, I speak at least one word of Irish every day. I was born in Belfast, Protestant by Tradition. But not British. And definitely not English. Not Irish, but Northern Irish. A north of difference. This wrestling with words is part and parcel of growing up on this island of Ireland, in the area known by some as Northern Ireland, with links to the British State and Crown, and known (nay, insisted on) by others as the North of Ireland – not recognizing the legitimacy of the British and their hold on this part of the island. But now I speak at least one word of Irish every day. It's this word: *Croí*. The Croí is probably my favourite building at the Corrymeela Centre. The Croí is not a church, and yet when the bell sounds twice a day, people are called to worship and reflect there. It is called, by some, the heart of the community. For others, it is a place of painful reminders (of church, of childhood) and a place to avoid. Who wants to face their fears twice a day – like some ill-considered exposure therapy? Added to that, who wants to face the truth in a place where the name of the Divine is called out, called upon, invoked and 'prayed to' on a twice-daily basis? Does that make the pain more or less bearable? I suppose it depends on who caused the pain and how we define the divine. And now I am happy to speak at least one word of Irish every day. For some, the naming of a place in Irish is an act of political provocation. For others, it's a banner of welcome. Language is important on this island, partly because the Troubles was a 'white-on-white fight', and we needed to find linguistic ways of recognizing the threats on our life, the 'enemy' in our midst. We asked: 'What's your name?' Looking out for Protestant/Catholic/British/Irish connections. We asked: 'What school did you go to?' Because most schools were, and still are, segregated along Catholic/Protestant lines.

We asked: 'What sport do you play?' We asked: 'Where do you live?' We were looking for the enemy in a sentence. We were trying to reduce the person to a sentence. A death sentence. The death of curiosity. The limiting of a person or safety-first linguistics? The lack of nuance or the only way to live in times of terror? Are there more than two ways to live? Lives beyond the binary? I am part of an arts collective called Thinkbucket. Our aim is to offer creative possibilities in community relations. In a region where so much is polarized, Thinkbucket seek to generate a diversity of perspectives and options *through imagining* in a different and complexity-inducing way. (Outside of the box. On top of the box. In a brightly repainted box. In a box broken up and made into a boat.) One day, the founder of Thinkbucket, a Corrymeela member, invited the collective to go on a trip – an open-top bus tour of Belfast. I am from Belfast. I thought – what am I going to learn about my home city? This is for tourists – it will either be partisan or partial or simplistic and glib. But it turned out to be something quite special, as we sat with a group of outsiders – British, German, Spanish – being given a witty commentary on the city I love. Everyone should go on an open-top bus

tour of where they live. View the familiar from a different perspective – in this case from high up on a bus, the
wind in my face, tourists all around, and a cheeky chap
giving out one-liners about the *Titanic*, the Troubles and
where to get a good pint. Anyway, the bus goes up the
Shankill Road, turns off into Tennent Street and then
stops at the bottom of Madras Street. And the tour guide
calmly says (in a counterpoint to the melodrama), 'This
is the heartland of Loyalism, the heartland of Protestant
paramilitaries.' He referenced British flags, Pro-British
murals, various street names. The passengers (tourists)
are suitably impressed and safely scared. But in my head
I am laughing and raging. In my head I am wanting to
shout out this: 'My granny lives on Madras Street! Her
name is Mary but people call her Min!' Behind every
grand statement is a granny. Language and its limits! And
I grew up hearing that the Shankill Road and the Irish
language were seemingly incompatible. The Shankill and
the Irish language? No!

Except that the name Shankill is from the Irish word
Seanchill, meaning 'old church'. And Belfast is from the
Irish word *Béal Feirste*, meaning 'river mouth of the
sandbanks'.

Oh, my word! I have been speaking Irish my whole
life! I have been surrounded by Irish since birth! Growing up, I would have been suspicious of a word I thought
was Irish (conditioned to suspicion). And now the Croí is
one of my favourite places. But for others it's still a place
with the language of the enemy attached to it. For those
declaring themselves Irish it's a delight to hear the word.
And for international visitors it's merely a foreign name
to mispronounce: 'I really love your Croy – your little
church – it's so adorable.' Humans are tuned to antici-
pate danger. Quiz time:

Question One – On hearing an Irish word, what do you do?
a) Tense up.
b) Relax.
c) Smile politely (but get ready to run).
d) (Other response).

Question Two – On hearing a bell sounding for worship, what do you do?
a) Swear loudly.
b) Smile politely (but swear inwardly).
c) Smile and give thanks.
d) Walk cautiously towards the Croí.
e) (Other response).

Question Three – Can humans be re-tuned?

At 9.30 am and 9 pm the bell rings. In the welcome speech, groups are told that this is the rhythm of the centre. For the non-religious it seems an archaic idea. For the religious it can be both a comfort and a challenge. Comfort, in that it may support and nurture them. Challenge, in that it may not fit with their version of the Divine. For those from other faiths it can be a challenge. They want to be polite. They are guests. They know what Corrymeela is. They are told that attending worship is optional, voluntary, but this is often not believed. Sometimes they think (and later tell me): 'You want to convert me, you want to change me.' When a Muslim asks to do Friday prayers there can sometimes be kick-back from certain Christians. And a Buddhist teaching meditation can also sometimes muddy holy waters.

But today I can say, after long twists and turns on the way, that I am happy to speak at least one word of Irish

every day. Perhaps this might be a reconciliation pre-
scription:

> On a daily basis, recite the words of an alien, an out-
> sider, a foreigner.
> Observe how they feel on the tongue.
> Seek out their various senses and tenses.
> Listen to how they chime or clang in your story.
> Notice where they pass or are stopped at your borders.

It's a beautiful day

Mira was special. Twenty-three, from Ramallah, Palestine, with an attitude that could fell a fat cat from a thousand yards. With a gentleness that could charm every stray kitten on-site. With a disorienting Palestinian-meets-Derry mash-up accent. Mira was politically redder than a ginger Marxist and had the red dancing shoes to prove it. Mira was a volunteer with us for 12 months, working as a programme assistant, working with Matt and Oona to make life-changing programmes. Or if not life-changing, then at least fun-filled and food-aplenty. And on second thought, aren't food and fun (and their lack) the materials for revolution?

It was a Tuesday morning, and Mira was on 'Cover'. Cover at the centre was taken on a rota basis, and was akin to that of being duty manager for a 24-hour period. The 'go-to' person. The person who gave tours to unscheduled guests. The person who held the building keys overnight, who ran to the scene of a plumbing malfunction. Blocked toilet? Call Cover. No toilet roll? Call Cover. It was a glamorous role. The person on Cover also gave the 'cover speech' to all participants new on-site, a speech that consisted of a Warm Welcome, a Safety Talk and Community Guidelines. And, as if all of that were not enough for one person, Cover also had another aspect. If there was no one signed up to do worship and reflection during that 24-hour period, then, guess what? It was down to the Cover person. It helped to have a reflection 'in your pocket' for an occasion such as this. The canny Cover people used their favourite reflective piece over and over. Sometimes it got better with repeated use. And of course, the audience was usually different. But there is a tricky dilemma with Cover having to cover what might be called a religious community activity. Sure, there was training for all aspects of Cover, but if you were not religious, or not Christian, or had been hurt by religion in the past, then it was a potentially compromising situation – for both the centre and the Cover person. There was no brief that the reflection had to always be Christian. There was no brief that the reflection had to always be religious. Worship Guidelines asked people to be aware of who was on-site, to make the reflection relevant if possible, to be aware that the person on Cover was representing an aspect of Corrymeela (and its reputation). The brief also encouraged brevity and preparation, and gave many examples of stories, music, scriptural texts, creative reflections, songs etc.

But the main requirement for doing a worship/reflection was that it be authentic – that it was honest and true for that person.

Mira was always transparent about her dislike of having to fill in the worship rota, and she rarely attended the Croí if she could avoid it. Unless one of her friends was doing something, and then she attended in solidarity to that person. And on this particular Tuesday, Mira came into the main building, looked at the worship rota for that day and saw that the 9.30 am slot was empty. I heard her mutter an expletive. An English expletive. (Mira could swear fluently in many languages.) I was about to intervene/offer support when she stomped off to concoct a reflection. Mira went out the front door to prepare: she lit a cigarette. Nothing like nicotine to get a person in the mood for leading a worship session. Karl Barth would have been proud (apparently Barth liked a good smoke as he reflected on the deep things of God). With her cigarette finished, Mira strolled off – in the opposite direction from the Croí – to Coventry (the volunteer house) where she lived on-site. At 9.25 am I walked slowly over to the Croí. The site is reminded of this community rhythm by the ringing bell, that clangs out a jolt to all. No bell had yet sounded out. At 9.30 am, the Croí is filling up. Corrymeela is famous for its flexible time-keeping. About ten people came in and took a seat in the circle. A few of the volunteers took a cushion and sat on the floor. At 9.32 am (I'm sorry, but when you are Centre Director you look at your watch a lot) I heard the bell ring outside. Ten seconds later Mira came in, a haze of curly black hair and cigarette odour. She fell on to the floor in front of the music system and plugged her I-pod into it with a large electronic *buzz!* The room was charged to attention. With her bum in the air, she pored through her music collection, either feeling inspired or looking for a spark to fill 15 minutes with meaning. Basic group-work would recommend greeting participants as early as possible in the process, perhaps as they entered and came into the space. Mira had read another group-work manual: *it will start when I am ready, and you will get what I give you.* The volume of conversation increased, as Mira ignored the room, kneeling (not praying) with her bum in the air. Shane, the Centre Manager, rolled his eyes at me and smiled. He was nervous. He had good cause to be. A week earlier, Mira had also covered Worship. She had played a Palestinian rap tune to a room full of Americans who kept their heads down and fumed or tried to become invisible, as they listened to the lyrics that spewed out the rappers' hate for US foreign policy. The chorus was in English, and went something like: *Oh, America, don't you know that the money you give kills innocent children. There's blood on your hands, children's blood on your hands. Oh, America!* Mira had prefaced her far-from-gentle tune by telling the invited that her former boyfriend had been arrested and tortured by the Israeli police. She was graphic in her description of what had occurred.

And here we were now, on this Tuesday morning, waiting for God knows what, with Mira all concentration, on the ground, kneeling (not praying), looking for something/anything? on her iPod. Suddenly a song: a few bars of a Bob Dylan song barked out. Then, just as suddenly, it was silenced. Mira remained on the floor, crouching on her knees, looking for some elusive mood music. Shane looked at me as if to say, *you are the Centre Director – do something!* But then Mira finds her voice. Her song. Her song for us today. 'Right', she says, 'this is a song by U2'. And then she presses PLAY and one of my favourite songs comes on. 'Beautiful Day' by U2. It's an optimistic tune with lyrics that jangle my soul to attention. The room atmosphere alters, going from tense to foot-tapping and big-smile faces. The music begins muted but rhythmic, a low treated piano sequence with some faraway strings. A patter of bass-drum patterns. The voice comes in quick, gentle, weary, soft. Bono sings about hearts opening, of powerful hearts bursting out of rough ground. And I don't know if it's my history with this song, with this band, but I feel my eyes begin to water. It's only a song, Paul. Catch yourself on. Bono is talking about tough times, and how we might live in them. And then Bono raises his voice into the chorus which literally says, 'It's a beautiful day', which on its own, sitting without melody or music, is quite a limp, banal phrase, quite a naïve chorus. But with a melody and the band, it's a wonder. It's a rousing charge of feeling beyond words. It's a drench of hope in a blast of sound.

The Edge is wailing a heart-felt '*Day*' on backing vocals. The lyrics in the verses are not clear about their direction or purpose, but the song is clearly moving me somewhere. Second verse and my emotions are rising. Bono finishes the verse describing a person's long high-low journey and the impact on their life. And his tone fills in the gaps of the oblique lyrics. 'You are covered in bruises and cuts from the tussle and delights of life', is how I translate the lyrics. And then that monster-big chorus again, this time with a longer section where Bono cries out for contact, for a new circumstance, to teach him, for love to reveal hope.

Who is he talking to? Can love be taught? Is he talking to a human love, to something Divine? (And might these things intermingle?) He asserts that he is desperate but not completely out for the count.

Mira is now standing by the music system, eyes closed, swaying slightly. And then the song breaks down, the drums fall away, and Bono does one of his lists lyrics:

He paints the world in blues and greens.

He mentions China – perhaps giving us a view from space of their famous wall, from on-high (from heaven?).

He digs out canyons in our minds.

He waves at ships destroying the sea.

He lights our imagination with flames in the desert (burning bushes, perhaps?).

He wails into life an image of oil fields at dawn.

And then he finishes with reference to Noah and the flood, focusing on the hope-high swoon of a bird carrying a leaf.

And of colours flooding the world with optimism after a deluge.

Bono is describing a broken, tortured, ugly, gorgeous world. And he is still singing about it being a beautiful day. And his biblical ending, with the flood story, Noah and the end of the world, and signs of a new world flying against the tide – a bird in motion carrying a beak of possibility. But right now, I leave aside the deep horror of the Noah story. Right now, I leave aside the scientific challenges of all those creatures together in a boat. Right now, I leave aside the lack of geological evidence for this story. Right now, Bono and Mira are leading me to a different place. This song doesn't make complete sense. Not head sense. This song is four minutes and eight seconds long and it is shouting to me: Don't let this bruising, beautiful, crashing, caressing day get away!

Mira pays heed to the lyric and stops the track before it begins to fade. Boldly stops it in all its glorious energy. She looks at us fiercely. Her chest rises as if she is filling her lungs to shout at us. She doesn't shout. But she does command us. 'Now,' she says. 'Go. Have a beautiful day.' And with that she turns her back to us, unplugs her iPod (another large buzz), and then she is walking out of the Croí. Mira is done. Mira is gone. In the dim light of the Croí, I make out smiles, stunned faces, confusion and serious frowns. But no one seems to be hanging about. They are taking Mira's words out into the day. Have a beautiful day. We have been sternly ordered to have a beautiful day.

Mira died three years later. In America. She had been protesting at an Occupy Washington event. She had outstayed her legal visa limit. She had taken ill and died suddenly. Heart attack. Only twenty-seven.

Mira was special.

Building a new heart

In the build-up to the building of the Croí, when funds were being raised, and temperatures were being gauged, a group of worthy weighty voices called for a stop to the plans for a new heart at Corrymeela. For them, to call a single place the heart was heartless. For them, to call the Croí *the* place of worship had great potential to halt the practice of worship wherever, to limit prayer to a single place. 'God cannot be contained!' they proclaimed. God cannot be held in a house of designated prayer! And so, the community prayed. For there was truth in the dissenting words. In the end, money was raised, fears assuaged, and dissent did not lead to division or distance. And the minority were not marked or marginalized.

The Croí was built with the proviso that the space should have multiple uses. That the Croí be used for play. That the Croí be used for parties. That the Croí be used for conference, debate and declaration. That the Croí be filled with prayer, pause and ponder. And that all of the hill and valley of life would be viewed as sacramental. That Croí could be found in every moment. And so, it was so.

Dreams (Part 1)

An old black Mercedes prides its way into our car-park.
Quite an entrance for the man who was to volunteer with
us for a year, but Ethan was always exploding expectations. Hailing from Denny in Scotland, Ethan brought
charm, pool-table hustle, haggis, and a new awareness
of disability rights. Mid-twenties. Big dreams. A brilliant
volunteer.

One Friday lunch-time he said: 'I've got a great idea
for worship tonight. You should come along.' I did.

Friday night worship was at 10 pm and, due to its later
start-time, it was usually an adult-only event, with kids
tucked up in bed and teenagers buzzing around the site,
high from drinking milky sugar, aka Hot Chocolate. I
arrived early to see Ethan wrestling with wires. His plan
was to show a speech from YouTube, but he couldn't get
the laptop and data projector to talk to each other. Outside, the bell rang to invite the people on-site to the Croí.
People would be arriving any second. Or not. Sometimes
Friday night worship was a solitary experience, with no
one turning up to hear your prepared profundity. But
people started to arrive. Ethan draws a crowd, charms
birds from trees. Volunteers piled in and gave encouraging *thumbs up* signs to Ethan, who was still head-down,
fiddling with wires and laptops. A group of women from
East Belfast arrived into the space with their children
in tow. The kids were saucer-eyed curious, fidgety and

kinetic (ranging in age from four to eleven). For most of
the kids, this was their first time in the Croí – this strange
Hobbit house with the sometimes-spooky acoustics. The
kids saw volunteers sitting on red cushions on the floor,
and bounced down beside them, talking about what they
saw:

'There's a candle, Mummy.'
'Can I touch the candle, Mummy?'
'Can I touch it?'
'Mummy – there's a box of matches.'
'Can I shake the matchbox, Mummy?'
'I'm only going to shake them.'
And the parents were nervous and laughing and count-
ing to the kids. Counting like this:
'I want you to put the matches down.'
'One.'
'Two …'
'This is your last chance before I …'
'Thank you.'
'Now sit and be quiet.'

But the kids were up late in a strange place with strangers
in a room with a candle flickering. And the kids loudly
talked what they saw:

'What's that book, Mummy?'
'Is this a church?'
'It's not?'
'Then why is there a Bible here?'
'Are you allowed to have a Bible in a place that isn't a
church?'
'Can we get a Bible for our house?'
'Why not?'

And a serious-faced girl said: 'I can tell you the names of the first and last books of the Bible.' I was impressed. 'Genesis and Revelation,' she said, with some pride. Ethan was still wrestling with the wires to the data projector. Technology is amazing. If it works. Ethan looked over at me and I raised my eyebrows to say: 'Are you OK?' He nodded.

But the kids were getting restless in a strange place with strangers in a room with a candle flickering. Time for a diversion. Plan P. I stood up and clapped my hands: 'OK, kids. It's good to see you tonight. And adults too, you are all very welcome to the Croí. Ethan is leading us in the session tonight, but his technology is playing up – it'll be ready in a second. But before that, let's play a game. What we are going to do is this. After I count to three, I want you to shout out your name. Do you think you can do that?' 'James!' shouts a seven-year-old who had not yet grasped the rules of the exercise. 'There you go! James here is showing us how fast he can shout his name. So, I want you to be really loud for me. Can you be loud for me?' 'Yes! I can!' shouted another small boy. And he could. 'OK, after three. Are you ready? Here goes. I will count to three and when we get to three, you all shout out your names, really loud, OK? Here goes. One two, (dramatic pause) three!' And the Croí fills with children's names being shouted happily at 10 pm on a Friday night, in a strange room with an Irish name. Did I mention the fact that all of these kids were from a staunch Protestant background? And that Irish was not a big feature on their landscape? I look over at Ethan. He is still struggling to get the clip to play large on the white curved wall of the Croí. I take the lack of image and sound from Ethan and his technology as a cue to continue my impromptu kids' session. The parents of the kids are happy if the kids are happy. The volunteers are (mostly) happy to join in 'action-games'. The regular adults in the room expect the unexpected. And the adults who are here for the first time? They look on, undecipherable.

I tease the kids, 'That was ... really quite quiet.' 'No way!' they shout. A small boy stands and raises a fist at me. I say, 'Let's do it again, only this time really shout. That was really not very loud.'

'Now maybe we should stand up this time.'

The kids jump up, ready to show me what loud is.

'Volunteers, maybe you could stand as well?' The volunteers rise from their red cushions. 'So, here goes. One, two (dramatic pause) ... three!' The room belts out a range of names, some familiar, some exotic-sounding. The volunteers are international.

'Now that was a bit better, but I think you could do it a bit louder.

And this time I want you to say your name four times.

So, if it was me, I would shout out: "Paul! Paul! Paul! Paul!"

So, has everybody remembered their name?'

'You're stupid!' says the boy with his fist in the air again. 'OK, here goes. One, two (dramatic pause) ... three!' A liturgy of names is confidently wailed out into the Croí. I love it. They love it. Ethan is still not ready. And Ethan also wants the kids to be still and to concentrate on a YouTube clip. Apparently in black and white. And I am making them hyper. Change tack. 'OK, everybody, now we are going to do the same thing – say your name four times, but this time we are going to say it really quiet, like a whisper, like this (in a whispered voice) "Paul, Paul, Paul, Paul."' And then we say our names quietly. And the kids have gone from hyper to hushed. They are becoming present to themselves and their surroundings. I am starting to sweat. Some of the younger kids suddenly look worn out and flop back on to the cushions or beside their mums. But Ethan is ready. I wonder how subdued the kids really are. It's a big ask. To ask kids to watch a speech from a clergyman from 1963. I hope this works, for Ethan's sake. For all our sakes. Ethan explains what he is going to do. 'A man is going to talk about his dreams. A man from a long time ago, from 1963. A man is going to tell us his dream.' The kids look up at the projected image of a man in a sober black suit, black tie and white shirt. He has short hair and a small pencil moustache. The kids wait for him to share his dream. This could be a nightmare of shouting out and fustling. Ethan presses 'Play' and the first line we hear the man say is: 'I am happy to join with you today in what will go down in history as the greatest demonstration for freedom in the history of our nation ...' This is some opening line. He is speaking to a large crowd. It is an outdoor event. The crowd roar their approval of this line. History is being made and they want to shout their AMEN to this moment. The kids in the Croí look on. So far, fidget-free. The man continues. He has the rhythms of a preacher. He seems confident, passionate but not deranged. He is speaking at the Lincoln Memorial in Washington DC, USA.

He talks about 'Negro' slaves who had been seared in the flames of withering injustice.

What wonderful language this is. But is this something these kids are going to be held by? I look around. Something of the man's voice and presence keeps the kids staring, stationary. The man raises his voice as he proclaims that they have come to Washington to, and I quote, 'Remind America of the fierce urgency of now.' What a phrase: 'the fierce urgency of now'. Repeat this phrase 50 times a day and see what happens, I think to myself:

the fierce urgency of now
the fierce urgency of now
the fierce urgency of now
the fierce urgency of now
the fierce urgency of now.

I have heard this speech many times before. But I am hearing it strange in this context of Croí-time Friday night, surrounded by Belfast families. The man starts to be explicit about his dream. He speaks without notes. 'I have a dream …' is how he starts each line. A dream about justice. A dream to fight the nightmare. A dream to waken up America! He mentions a dream he has for children. I look at the kids watching a clip of a man talking about dreams from 1963. I wonder what they are hearing. I wonder if this moment will be remembered years later as the time when something about justice lodged in their souls. The man says, 'I have a dream that little children will one day live in a nation where they will not be judged by the colour of their skin but by the content of their character.' And in my head, I add: *and that they will not be judged by where they come from, their religion, their class, their rough accent, their impoverished east of Belfast.* And I am identifying with these kids and with this speech. I am also an East Belfast boy, smashed out of my family home at the age of ten. I feel my eyes starting to water. And the man changes his mantra, brings out a new slogan, a new catchphrase. He says, 'Let freedom ring!' as he names a variety of contexts. And he is filling up with pride and passion as he raises up his voice and proclaims: 'When we allow freedom to ring, when we let it ring from every village and hamlet, from every state and every city, we will be able to speed up that day when all of God's children, black men and white men, Jews and Gentiles, Protestants and Catholics, will be able to join hands and sing in the words of the old Negro spiritual, "Free at last! Free at last! Thank God Almighty, we're free at last!"'

Protestant and Catholics joining hands? Where does this man think he is? Corrymeela?

But what a speech, and strangely, how it held the room. 'Now, dreams are important,' says Ethan, turning off the big image of the man who was talking about freedom dreams. Ethan talks about all the dreams he has – of visiting a long list of countries – across the continent of Africa in particular. He talks about wanting to 'make a difference' – that odd, almost clichéd phrase.

'So, who has a dream about what they want to do when they grow up?'

Ethan is addressing the kids. The kids are taking centre stage. I am thinking to myself – this won't work – they are only kids. Their hands shot up like arrows at Agincourt. 'Me! Me! Me!' they shout. These kids have dreams. 'What do you want to be?' Ethan points at each raised hand. 'A footballer.' *(Great.)* 'A soldier.' *(You need to be fit for that.)*

'A hairdresser.' *(Handy.)* And then there were the two sisters, eight and ten years of age (I later found out). The elder sister spoke first, with a very serious face on her: 'I'd like to be a doctor and help poor children in Africa.' Her mummy nodded with pride, mouthing to her neighbours – 'this is true – she does – she's very thoughtful'.

'What a lovely dream,' says affirming Ethan. And then her younger sister, who is smiling like a little angel, loudly proclaims her big dream: 'I'd like to be a barmaid and pull pints for people.' Her mother laughs hysterically. 'Nice,' says Ethan. 'Two dreams involving helping people.'

And then it's time to wrap up. Ethan thanks everyone for coming, especially the kids.

The volunteers rise from their cushions, modelling that it's time to leave the Croí.

The parents stumble out with smiles on their faces, happy to have heard about their children's dreams, and perhaps touched by the speech made by Martin Luther King all those years ago. I remain seated. Ethan looks over at me, mimes wiping his brow. 'That was good,' he said. I nod agreement. 'Do you need a hand tidying up?'

'If you wouldn't mind unplugging the leads from the data projector that would be great. I can't reach it from my chair.' Ethan wheels himself around the Croí, sorting out equipment, smiling at what had just happened. He has let freedom ring – into the ears of children and adults, into the global ears of the volunteers, into the ears of a doubting Centre Director. I wonder if Ethan is wondering how being a wheelchair-user might affect his dreams. Perhaps it will be the very thing that propels him into his imagined future. Vulnerable, determined, gifted, dreaming. A few years later, Ethan was in Kenya, letting freedom ring.

Dreams (Part 2)

One year later I led another contemplation on dreams, using a song by a musical collective called One Giant Leap. Centred around two British electronica musicians/songwriters, their idea was to take a series of musical sketches/themes and then to travel the world, inviting a range of musicians to join in the creative act. They made a film and CD about their adventures. The result was a rich mix of contributors – singing, playing, talking about life, our connectedness, the issues facing us today. Their overarching theme was unity through diversity. Some of the people involved were

Dennis Hopper (famous for playing psychopathic killers in films)
Kurt Vonnegut (of *Slaughterhouse Five* fame)
Eddie Reader
Brian Eno (a hero of mine)
Neneh Cherry (an early crush)
Anita Roddick
Baaba Maal
Michael Franti
Robbie Williams (it's not all good)
And Michael Stipe.

Now Michael Stipe could sing the instructions on a paint tin and his voice would move me. And on this project, he

is 'singing to be heard', having started his career deliber-
ately mumbling about fragments of his life. In the song
that I play in the Croí, he is singing about dreams. The
song begins with a cryptic (and unknown to me) voice
gently encouraging us to practise being silent in order to
experience the Divine.

Then an acoustic guitar slowly picks out a simple
melody. Joining this simple guitar, a beautiful fluid
entrancing melody line, in the form of a female voice (the
Bollywood superstar, Asha Bhosle). I have no idea what
the words are. Is this the sound of dreams? Is this the
language of heaven in India? It is beautiful, made more
mysterious by its exotic lack of translation. (She could be
singing about a piece of toast she enjoyed.) Perhaps best
not to know. I have asked the assembled in the Croí to
focus on the song, the feel of the song, and especially the
chorus, which is 'I love the way you dream'. Repeated
and repeated and repeated by Michael Stipe. He sounds
in love with the person he is singing to. It sounds like an
intimate conversation put to song.

I ask the assembled to listen and wait. To see what
comes to mind. The song goes from Michael to Asha,
from English to Hindi, from familiar to unknown words.

The song increases in volume, rhythm, bends and
folds. And then I press 'Pause', and ask the group, 'What
do you think?' about a piece of music I adore. Risky.
I cannot force them to think or feel anything. I could
shape the conversation by saying how much I love this
song. But I hold back. Folk seem underwhelmed by the
song. A few know of REM, the band that Michael Stipe
played with, and reference other songs they like. But not
this one. The silence between statements is growing. I
give my reflections. I say, 'I am not sure what this song
is about. But I am imagining that this is God talking to
us, to the world. That the Divine she/he is singing this

over our lives. The Divine is saying "I love the way you dream." Over and over and over. For me it is an affirmation of us as humans, whatever our tradition or creed or allegiance or doubts. This is God saying, "I put many of those dreams/desires inside of you." Maybe not the dreams of world domination or sex with supermodels or getting a red Ferrari (although even those desires have something to take note of in their distorted cries for control, intimacy and value).' I finish talking. The room falls to silence. Perhaps this is too big a leap for the room, for the assembled. The conservative Christians in the room appear unconvinced, perhaps even taking note of yet another suspect statement of heresy or blasphemy (whatever fits). The atheists are having trouble making this connect to them, as they don't believe in a Divinity. And the other Traditions? Who knows? But I say it anyway. And I continue, because this song is, at the very least, impressing on *me* that God loves the way I dream. And that is frightening and delighting me in a churning disorienting way. God loves the way I dream. I say, 'I'm going to play the song again, and if you are so inclined, imagine that the Divine is saying to you, to you personally – "I love the way you dream". And for those of you struggling with this theology, take it as someone saying that your dreams, your deepest desires, your barely formed ambitions, are valuable, are worthwhile, and need to be nourished. Let this song nourish our dreams.' More silence. A few faces in the room look like I have just given them ten gigantic numbers to add up in their heads. I put the song on again.

'I love the way you dream,' sings Michael Stipe.[4]

'I love the way you dream,' says God in the voice of Michael Stipe.

My inner monologue is rambling – *Do you really love my dreams? Really? I get this. I sort of get this. I get this a little.* I stop the song and offer a closing blessing. People file out. No one says 'well done' or 'that was great'. They file out. I remain. I have a business meeting in 15 minutes. I feel opened up to a love that might make me cry, that might make me soft, tender. How am I going to get through the day feeling like this? And then, another thought – how am I going to get through the day, in a peace and reconciliation centre, if I don't live this openly? A crack has been opened. *I love the way you dream …*

Blindfolding an Iraqi

(A prose poem)

The Iraqi is anxious, waiting,
shivering as she stands in the dimly lit cave.
This Iraqi has a name.
Lubna.*
Its meaning is a mystery to the others in the room.
Lubna is standing, feet two feet apart,
arms placed tight against her side.
A blindfold is being placed over her eyes.
A black blindfold
that has been well used, many times,
to take the light from blinking eyes.

Lubna is from Baghdad.
Ancient city devastated
by American weapons in the name of peace.
In the name of killing the tyrant.
In the name of finding Weapons of Mass Destruction.
Using real weapons
to NOT FIND
Weapons of Mass Destruction.

Lubna is a thirty-four-year-old woman.
She is anxious, waiting,
shivering as she stands in the dimly lit cave.

I cannot imagine what Lubna has seen and met
in the blind-alley of her memory.

The blindfold is being placed over her eyes by a
physically fit American.
This American
runs marathons for fun, was home-schooled,
loves the *Lord of the Rings* and the Lord Jesus Christ.
This American asks, 'Can you see anything?' in her
American English.
Lubna replies in the negative with a shake of her dark-
    maned head.
Lubna is from Baghdad.
She speaks fluent English with a Liverpool accent
where she learnt her English,
jostling with the Liver Birds and the Mersey Sound and
the Anfield Roar
and Beatle chords.
She nods, answers without noise.

Lubna is far from Baghdad, waiting, shivering.
Shivering as she stands in the dimly lit cave.

Something new
is about to happen.
Something is about to happen
that has never happened to Lubna before.

The American waves a hand in front of Lubna's face,
to double-check for sight, for sure.
The American is also female.
This
physically fit American,
who runs marathons for fun, was home-schooled,
loves the *Lord of the Rings* and the Lord Jesus Christ.

This American is called Tiffany.** Two F's one Y.
I had never met a Tiffany
before I met this Tiffany.

And this Tiffany
was an original.

And this Tiffany has blindfolded three other people.
And I am one of them.
That's how I know what happened.
Because I was there,
when the American blindfolded the room, took away
our sight,
and gifted us a sacred moment.

That's how I know this story.
Because I was there. And I am back there again,
doing something wrong,
something against the rules of the room
as set by this American called Tiffany.

I am peeking out of my blindfold.
I have decided to cheat on the American called Tiffany.
This physically fit American,
who runs
marathons for fun,
was home-schooled, loves the *Lord of the Rings* and the
Lord Jesus Christ.

And I would do it again, break the rules, peek out,
because what I saw I loved,
In all its strangeness and never-again-to-be-replicated.
I am peeking out from my black blindfold,
squinting at Tiffany
who has

her back turned to me, and so
can't see
what I can:
Lubna,
standing, shivering with anticipation, blindfolded,
waiting, longing.
As she stands in this dimly lit cave.

As I recall it,
there were two other Nationalities in the room –
Hungarian and Irish.
These women wear the same black blindfolds, but are
smiling.
Perhaps they are more comfortable being led than I am.
Being led by an American.
By an American called Tiffany, who the blindfolded
women call Tiff.

Tiffany has had
a bold, oddly shaped idea.

Tiffany loves to dance and run and jump and climb and
leap,

and she has made a suggestion in this space.
And this oddly shaped idea mingles with the traces
of ten thousand other strange ideas that have been
uttered and ushered into this dimly lit space.

And this cave is the Croí.

And this is Corrymeela – the oldest peace and
reconciliation centre in Ireland,
an open Christian community, committed to
reconciliation.

And the Croí is not a Christian church,
and yet
Christians pray here.
And the Croí is not a mosque,
and yet
Muslims pray here.
and the Croí is not a synagogue,
but Jews
come to pray here.
And the Croí looks a bit like a chapel,
and Atheists come and talk about
'something more than flesh and blood',
without having to say,
'I am a believer in your God.'

We are all believers in something.

And Tiffany believes that today
blindfolds will reveal a blessing.
She explains:
'Sometimes you can't find the words.
You can't find the words
to form a prayer.
Praying to God takes many forms.
Sometimes all we have is silence.
Sometimes we recite
other people's words,
the words of the long-dead
bringing life.
But sometimes prayer is a dance,
a body moving, a life in motion.'

And we had all
agreed to try
this Incarnational Jig.

In Tiff we trust.

And the blindfolds were there
to keep us
from ourselves,
from embarrassment,
from looking at others (and comparing or competing).

This time was between us
and God.

And Tiff had put on some dance music – I remember
voices in Spanish,
chanting along to a slinky beat.

'Begin,' said Tiff.
'Don't peek.
Just feel the music and go.
Move.'

Lubna is far from Baghdad, waiting.
shivering as she stands in the dimly-lit cave of the Croí.

Don't peek.
I had to.

I had to break the rules.
I had to look, to bear witness,
to watch the weeping Lubna dance.

Call it betrayal if you want,
but I did not
turn to stone when I gazed at Lubna

swaying
to the rhythm. Moving slowly at first,

her tears more urgent than her limbs.
And then her arms rose up, higher, higher, and her body
pushed on and out and further, and faster, on.

Lubna leaves tomorrow, makes her way
back to Baghdad,
back to that ancient city in ruins.

And Tiffany has given
Lubna a gift.
This
physically fit American,
who runs marathons for fun, was home-schooled,
loves the *Lord of the Rings* and the Lord Jesus Christ.
Tiffany. Two F's one Y:
The gift of prayer without speech.
The gift of prayer whose sound is
the creaking of joints
the 'in' of breath
the 'out' of breath
the padding of feet on a carpeted floor
the flap of clothes on a moving form.

The gift of prayer in a cradle of unknowing.

And Tiffany is graceful and unashamedly tearful,
moving to a rhythm all her own,
confident in the home of her skin,
in the pulse of her heart;
a blessing of foot-taps, scuffs and lifts.

The American and the Iraqi dance.
Separate, together.
And I am dancing too, badly, with one eye squinting
from under my blindfold,

feeling in the presence of angels, messengers of the Divine.

*Lubna was a volunteer who lived and worked at Corrymeela for two months.
**Tiffany was one-half of the Resource Team, and volunteered at Corrymeela for nearly three years.

Cowboy in the Croí

He has manners. His Cowboy hat is always removed before going into the Croí. He is a well-mannered Texan. He is an actual Cowboy. His Cowboy hat is not an affectation. It is a sign of his culture, his roots. He is also a Catholic. A Catholic Cowboy sitting waiting in the Croí. His hat sits on the seat beside him. He waits with a heavy book in his hand and the reflection of a lit candle in his eyes. On-site today, a gathering of peace activists, academics, former combatants, ex-police. There is a marquee tent where the welcome and introductions are being made. One of the announcements during the opening of the peace conference:

> The book *Lost Lives* (containing stories of the men, women and children who died as a result of the Northern Ireland Troubles) will be read out every day in the Croí from 10 am to 5 pm. We do this to remember the dead. We do this to remember the loss. We do this to inspire us into a more flourishing non-violent future. Andy Hill will be leading these sessions. He is easy to spot. He is the only person on-site wearing a Cowboy hat.

This announcement, offered to a scrum of peace activists, who have dedicated their lives to the promotion of peace and reconciliation. This announcement, offered to a throng of academics who have studied our bloody past. This announcement, offered to people with family members in the book *Lost Lives*. This announcement, offered to people who have killed for a cause, and put people into the book *Lost Lives*.

Andy waits alone in the Croí. His hat sits on the seat beside him. He waits with a heavy book in his hand and the reflection of a lit candle in his eyes. If no one comes he will read all day, or read until his voice cracks and dies (he is committed). People come.

To listen. To honour. To grieve. To bear witness.
To read from the book *Lost Lives*.
To weep.
To pray.
To seethe and ache.

The book begins in 1966, with the death of John Scullion, aged twenty-eight, a store-man by profession.

The book ends in 1999, with the death of Charles Bennet, aged twenty-two, a part-time taxi driver.

There are 3,632 names recorded in the book *Lost Lives*. Today, an outsider leads the lament.

Ark in the heart

The large section of the Croí is jostling with movement, bodies, loudness; arrivals into the space – awkward running; slow clunking shuffles; two people pushed in wheelchairs; bellowing voices talking about food, dancing, shoes, haircuts. L'Arche are staying the weekend at Corrymeela. Founded by Jean Vanier, L'Arche is a group of communities set up around the world for people with learning disabilities. The differently-abled. Maria is the L'Arche leader in Ireland, and she is a holy disturber of my peace. She is small in stature, warm of welcome, penetrating with her seemingly simple questions. I love to see Maria, and she makes me slightly nervous. I am put off-balance by her personal open-ness, her earthy laugh and her direct gaze and too-long pauses.

It is the morning worship and reflection time. Maria is leading this. It is due to start at 9.30 am. It is 9.35 am and people are still arriving, loudly, creating a blessed rumpus. At 9.40 am, Maria welcomes everyone in the room. The Croí is far from what I would call 'settled' – members of the L'Arche community are still boisterously talking about the weather, their shoes, breakfast. The room is unsettled. No. I am unsettled. The 'norms' are being recalibrated. Maria seems oblivious to the ambience of shuffles, conversations and someone happily (burpingly) enjoying a can of Coke. Or else Maria is completely aware, very present to all that is going on in the room, and she is comfortable with it. I think, *If you have come today for a gentle, quiet reflection, you won't find it here*. And yet, there is gentleness everywhere. Calm responses to questions. An abundance of smiles. Hands softly held. Faces leaning in, intimately facing each other. It is so publicly, unguardedly, messily *raw*!

And today I am feeling the pressure of being Director, having been tasked by Corrymeela to increase lettings income, decrease expenditure and innovate new programmes of reconciliation. Bed-sheets, spread-sheets, score-sheets. Maria asks me to stand beside her. She tells the gathered: 'This is Paul. He is the Leader here. Say Hello.' They do, shouting 'Hello, Paul!' in sincere cacophony. Then it's time for an action song. I have no recollection of the tune or the words, only a series of unco-ordinated arm-movements and loud, proud, passionate singing. A heavenly discord? An earthly din? Then Maria addresses the Croí. She says: 'We are not enough.' Just like that. She says it again: 'We are not enough.' Why would she say this? On a day when I feel so *not enough*?

Why would she say such an uncomforting statement? It's true, of course. I do feel that I am not enough – that I won't be able to increase income, decrease expenditure and innovate new programmes. What if the job is too much for anyone? What if expectations are unrealistic? What if this quiet introvert is not up for the very public role of Centre Director? I had bowed my head with the weight of this statement. When I look up again, most of the room are nodding in agreement and smiling. Smiling! What is the matter with these people?! Well, perhaps the members of L'Arche hear 'You are not enough' every day by a society fixated on perfection, by an ill-informed media, by embarrassed family members, by standard education, by tutting shop-assistants, by impatient bus-drivers. This is what they know: that they are not enough if measured against 'societal norms'. And me? I don't want to admit my weakness, frailties, mistakes, blemishes. So, I hide them away.

The theologian David F. Ford, speaking at an Anglican conference I attended in 2017, suggested that if society placed the rich, powerful, beautiful people at its centre, then at some point we would all be excluded. But, says Ford, if we placed at the centre of society those with learning disabilities, children, the elderly, then we could all find a place, a welcome, inclusion. A world upside down.

Jean Vanier, in the opening pages of his profound book *The Broken Body*, says that we find the love of the Divine through making 'a covenant of love with the poor, the weak and the oppressed'.[5] Vanier urges us 'not to run away from people who are in pain or who are broken, but to walk towards them. Then you will find rising up within you the well of love, springing from resurrection. And when we do this we will meet our own brokenness, our own darkness. But that Jesus is hidden in this brokenness, this poverty, this oppression.'

But at this moment, in this raucous and smiling gathering, I am struggling to accept this. I am habituated to push this truth away. I want to cry but hold it in. I have taught myself to 'hold it in'. It takes so much energy to 'keep it in'. How do I go back to my precise, unyielding spread-sheets after this? Keep it in. Push the truth away. Cover the truth with spread-sheets.

And then Maria goes further, because her message was not finished (it's already too far). Maria says: 'We are not enough ... on our own. But together we are enough. Not perfect. Not complete. Not fixed. But together we are enough.' No! It's hard enough saying I am not enough. Now you want me to share this truth with someone? But if I don't share it, I am on my own. I have made myself alone. But who can I trust with all these unacceptable truths about myself?

Maria continues: 'The solution is all around us. Together we are enough. And who you are is enough, because it's all you have. All you have is enough. All you have is loved.'

All I have is enough? All I have is loved? My face is suddenly wet. I am crying in public. I want to be simultaneously invisible and noticed. And then something else. A rare prayer. A vigorous rocker in a wheelchair sways too far, falls out of her creaking wheelchair with a spectacular flop, hitting the floor with an impressive *thwump!* And, as she hits the floor, a huge sound pushes out of her, forming the words:

'Oh, Jesus!!!!' It's shocking – the fall; the calling out; the lying on the floor; the naked need of the prayer. I watch Maria glance over, to check if the assistant has seen the incident (she has), and then continue. But I am not listening to what Maria says next, because the voice in my head is shouting: *Pick her up! Get her up! Get her back in her wheelchair!*

But no one is rushing to assist. No one is rushing to 'fix' the situation. Then this: the assistant of the woman who has fallen, responds. She doesn't pick her up. Instead, she lies down on the floor *with* the person who has fallen. No! Get up! Both of you get up! Now there's two of you lying there on the ground! And then this: the assistant leans in, whispers something I can't hear, and then slowly, gently, begins to stroke the fallen woman's hair. With great care and attention. She connects to her fallen friend, stays grounded, floored, visible to the world, close to the feet of others who are moving with dangerous flicking abandon. This is a health and safety nightmare *and* we are not enough. We are not enough on our own. What we have is enough. What we have is loved.

Eventually, the L'Arche session in the Croí ends and I make a quick exit. I have no idea how long it took to get the lady back into her wheelchair. What if she stayed there for ever? Loved where she fell. Loved in her un-fixed state. Held in a tender gaze. Unmoored and connected in a chorus of lost and found.

Let there be a new saint to entreat:

Lady tumbling
from your wheelchair,
preserve me in my falling.

Lady lying on the floor,
save me through my weakness.

Lady of the earnest swear-prayer,
open my lips to honest speech.

Lady of the gently stroked hair,
guide my mind when stressed and harried.

Amen

TOGETHER

Living reconciliation
(a dozen glimpses)

01. Devotions

Most Thursdays you can see a small group of community members bow low and touch the earth. They wear rough clothes and do what they do in silence. Small talk is exchanged with passers-by, but there is a feeling that this polite conversation is getting in the way of something more important. They are faithful to the particularity of their vision. They move across the whole of the Corrymeela site, seasonally shifting their tasks – slowly, methodically, earthily. They see Corrymeela from a different perspective. All over sixty in age, they stoop and lean and wrestle with creation. They dig and pull and cut and sweep. They are aware that the ground holds life and death. They sow seeds, uproot. And only occasionally do they impatiently exclaim that tending to the land is the first priority of every person. That everything else comes second to this. Behold the grass growing.

~

02. Good practice

There are days when I resist the call to the Croí when
the bell rings for worship. Not because I have too much
work – there is always too much work. Not because it's
a loud, action-based children's worship that is planned.
And not because it's raining. No. There are days I resist
the call to the Croí because I know who will be there.
Someone I have disagreed with, have possibly hurt (consciously or not). I don't want to be a hypocrite, paint a
smile and say the prayers. I don't want to go through
the motions because I am in conflict with someone, a
complex conflict that is unlikely to go away quickly.
But anticipated discomfort in the Croí is not a reason
to avoid it. There may be a learning in the discomfort.
There may be found a healing, a resilience, a suppleness,
an insight. And it's good practice: disagreeing and not
fleeing. And it's good practice: recognizing the conflict
in a relationship, and trying to define the relationship as
bigger than the conflict.

~

03. Cameroon

At the induction of new one-year volunteers we talk
again and again about the word 'community'. We talk
about it because we think it's important. We underline
the connectedness of work and relationships, between
free-time and work, between visitors and ourselves. For a
certain volunteer from Cameroon this was heard as 'I can
take whatever I like from the community fridge.' This
behaviour was tolerated for a week before fights started.

   'But this is someone else's food – they paid for it,' I
said.

'But this is the community fridge,' he said. 'But they have put their name on it,' I said. 'We don't lose our names in community – we share,' he said.

We strongly disagreed on the definition of 'community'. And we agreed that certain behaviours, like taking someone else's food without asking was not appropriate in *this* community. And when I say *agreed*, I mean that I told him it was not appropriate and that it needed to stop. After six months 'in community' with us, this charming Cameroonian disclosed what he really thought and felt about living in the Corrymeela community: 'Everyone in the West is rich,' which explained a lot of his seemingly unrepentant behaviour about taking stuff: I am a poor Cameroonian. You are a rich Westerner. You can afford it. This is justice when I take the food, ask for money. This is justice, not a crime. This is what I heard him say. To be accurate, the above phrase is what I heard him say behind what he actually said, which was this: 'I don't understand, Paul. My English not yet good.' Hearing can be seriously impaired if you are a liberal, guilt-haunted, do-gooding Westerner running a peace centre in Ireland.

~

04. A list of names

The Corrymeela Prayer Guide has a month of daily readings, topics to pray for. And a list of names in alphabetical order – community members, staff, volunteers. We are encouraged to remember these names, these people, on a particular day each month, to hold them up in prayer. To regard them.

It's easier to pray if I like the person and am currently getting along with them. It makes it difficult (and even more necessary) to pray if the person named is someone I don't naturally relate to, or is a person I have been hurt by, or am in conflict with. But this is why the list is important. It holds us to the task of reconciliation. And teaches us how to pray in a larger way, in a way that is bigger than (but still acknowledges) our hurts and likes/dislikes.

And so, some days I pray in blindness, knowing that there is something beyond my feelings for that person, but not being able to see it. Sometimes I stumble at these names, stop praying and start re-living the drama that caused injury. Sometimes I have been the perpetrator. And sometimes I pray like this:

> The spirit of the Lord is on me,
> because I have been called to proclaim good news
> to my inner broken longing self.
> I have been placed here before these names,
> at this place,
> at this time,
> to announce the possibility of freedom for my own imprisoned life.
> I have been placed here before these names,
> at this place,
> at this time,
> to name my own blindness,
> and that recovery of sight is possible, immediately or slow.
> I have been placed here before these names,
> at this place,
> at this time,
> to say that
> there is a cure for my oppression,
> to say that
> there is a healing repentance
> for my own oppressor tactics.
> I have been placed here before these names,

at this place,
at this time,
to receive the notice that Jubilee is here:
debts repaid
forgiveness received
justice served
mercy flowing.
(After Luke 4 vv. 17–19)

And several times a year I receive in the post an envelope, bearing familiar flowing handwriting. And inside, a hand-made card. I know exactly who it's from. And I smile and give thanks even before I read the card. The card that tells me that at least one person in the world has remembered me for at least a few moments on that day of the month. A huge faithfulness embodied in a modest personalized card.

Thank you, Mathilde.

~

05. Where is the Jew?

The email began with a line that was hard to resist: 'I am a pilgrim walking from Berlin to Jerusalem.' I read on. He was a German. He had sent a newsletter with two images of himself – one with lots of hair and the other where he was cue-ball bald. He was walking from Berlin, his home city, stopping off at peace sites/centres, and also some of the Nazi death camps dotted across Europe. He was on a pilgrimage for peace. He was currently in Iona, Scotland. Could he come and stay at Corrymeela Peace Centre? His name was Elijah. Very biblical. I put my deep curiosity aside and replied with requests for practical details: when he would like to come, and for how long, etc. Then nothing. No reply, acknowledgement or hint of having received my message. We get weekly requests for people to stay at Corrymeela. We are on the Pilgrim Map, which typically has three intersecting co-ordinates: alternative holiday, spiritual searching, convenient toilet-stop. I forgot about him.

Five days later there is a knock on the door at Corry-meela. It's a Friday night, 10.45 pm. And a seven-foot-one man with a shaved head is staring in through the glass door at Coventry, our volunteer accommodation. It is Elijah. The door is opened by Valentine, a very different type of German: eighteen, tanned, dark-haired, pleasant, tall, sporty. Valentine is one of our long-term volunteers. He greets Elijah warmly, but asks who he is and what he wants. Elijah says that he is from Germany. They change language and continue the conversation in their mother tongue. Elijah says that he has contacted the Centre Director, whose name he can't remember. Valentine offers refreshment, and goes to get a staff member. Eli-jah is given a room for the night. As the story unfolded, it seems that Elijah was on the ferry from Scotland to Ireland, and had asked the person standing next to him on deck if he knew where Ballycastle was (where our centre is located). It is now legend that the man replied that he was taking a full load of something (we missed this detail) in his van to Ballycastle. He offered Elijah a lift. How do you unravel this? Ask enough people and eventually someone will be going to Ballycastle? Ask God to provide and he does? What do we learn from the times he doesn't provide? Or are we to call this *mystery*, and leave it at that? The first person Elijah asked gave him a lift straight to our door.

The next morning I am part of a community residential weekend, looking at the work of René Girard and his theory of Scapegoating. There are around 60 community members on-site. A tall man in walking boots and rough outdoor clothing is guided to me. Elijah. He is carrying a candle, given to him by the Iona Community, his previous hosts. The candle is at least 15 inches long. Never in my life have I been afraid of a candle. Until now. Elijah brandished his candle, holding it tight and upright at his waist, nearly head-height for mere mortals. He held it like a weapon, as if the enemies of peace could be dispatched with a crack to the cheek or a poke in the side or a rap on the knuckles. This giant candle-wielding German loomed over me and introduced himself. I smiled and shook his non-candle hand, welcomed him, and asked why he had not replied to my email. (We are hospitable at Corrymeela, but not push-overs. Generous but discerning. We welcome strangers 50 weeks of the year, but we try to do it with wisdom and boundaries.) Elijah was frank. (This was to be a motif of our conversation.) He said that he never phones ahead in case people thought he was mad. And yet turning up in the middle of the night unannounced is sane? 'Let's talk about how long you are staying. What about you stay until Monday?'

To which Elijah replied: 'No. I think Tuesday.'

Now at this point his blunt second-language English has got under my skin. What to do? Insist on Monday? Leave it as Tuesday? I agreed to Tuesday, but outlined some of the community guidelines. At that moment, another German walked past: Sonja, our volunteer support worker. I stopped her in her tracks and introduced Elijah. I asked her to sit down with him and go through community life. She did so firmly and kindly.

Elijah was keen to sit in on the theology sessions. He sat bolt upright, mirroring the 15-inch club-like candle in his hand. I introduced him to the room. He asked if he could light the candle. It was not appropriate at that time, given the nature of the conversation. He sat to attention with his attention-grabbing garb and height.

When I came back to the room 20 minutes later, the candle was lit and sitting on the table in the middle of the room. It's hard to argue with a giant German and his spear-candle. I was not warming to this man. Unlike the candle, which was dripping hot wax on to the table. My health and safety head was on red-alert.

Throughout the day, Elijah received lots of attention. We encourage curiosity at Corrymeela, and it's hard to ignore someone that size. Some people stared, others approached his exotic-ness, stirred by his pilgrimage, feeling land-locked, fixed, conservative, cosy, mortgaged, family-fretted. He asked to deliver a 20-minute slide show on his journey. I said No, it was not appropriate. Maybe later with the volunteers.

Elijah, uncertain of his words or just bad-blunt, had heard there was someone from a Jewish heritage living at Corrymeela, and blurted out loudly: 'Where is the Jew?', causing both consternation and concern in the five-foot-one female volunteer he had spoken to. Maybe it was the fact that Elijah was two feet taller than she was. Maybe it was his tone of voice. Anyway, she went and found Yael and told her the Teutonic tale. The Jew was not amused. Eventually Elijah met 'The Jew' and said: 'Hello, can we talk about the Holocaust?' Yael paused, considered the request, and then said: 'No.' And walked off without an explanation. There is no obligation for the only Jew at Corrymeela to listen to a German talking about the Holocaust.

Elijah did not get his conversation with Yael about the Holocaust. But he did get to deliver his slide-show to the volunteers. Volunteers from Cameroon, various parts of the USA, the Philippines, Hungary, England and Ireland. And Valentine (pronounced valen-teen) from Germany. The volunteers were pitched the slide-show as an uplifting and heart-cleansing pilgrimage of peace.

What they got was a guilt-ridden, doom-laden, hair-shirt presentation of European death camps, interspersed with the occasional flickering light of a peace centre. The emphasis was clearly on death, starkly on Elijah and his bleeding journey. Most wanted to leave after 20 minutes, but politely held on for another hour of provocation and soul-corroding guilt. And, because walking for peace is a 'worthy' thing to do, the volunteers allowed themselves to be subjected to this guilt-attack, this 50-gravity feeling of heaviness. Some worthy causes have done great harm in this world. Worthy causes do not guarantee purity of process. But we often desire our heroes to be one-dimensional and pure, single-minded and sexy or sexless, dedicated and perfect. And when we scrutinize our heroes, and see them as human in all that that means – frail, wonderful, passionate, wounded, guided and lost – we still get disappointed and then angry at their imperfections, their human-ness. Idolatry is a common default position. Elijah seemed to me a big gesture for peace that seemed devoid of the small mercies of attention to the wonderful minutiae of what is present before us at every moment. Sure, there are epic and defining moments, and grand heroic acts, but family life thrives on the heroic attention to the everyday, the dinner money, the homework, the gentle kiss on the cheek, bodies finding each other in the night and relearning how things fit. Most of life is about dealing with the small things.

On Tuesday, Elijah gathered himself publicly in the lobby of the main building. He ceremonially packed his warm clothes, and hung various objects on to a rucksack the size of a single bed. Corrymeela makes a big deal about welcomes and goodbyes. We work hard at this. However, today, no one wanted to 'see him off', as they say in these parts. I was the only person who stood and watched as he robed himself in his layers of waterproof self-righteousness. I felt guilty – I found this man a struggle. After arriving unannounced on Friday evening, Elijah had been given food and room until Tuesday. And not once had he said *thank you*, or given us a single penny for his stay. And as I waited for him to depart, I grew angry. Is Elijah abusing us? Or is this the code of a peace pilgrimage? He paid for nothing, offered his gargantuan guilt and slide-show, and thanked us for nothing.

'I will give some of these extra clothes to people I meet on the road,' intoned Elijah.

It's good to travel light, I thought, but Elijah is a heavy pilgrim. I gave Elijah gifts for his journey – two tokens from our shop – a notebook adorned on the front with a candle image, and a plastic poncho that probably wouldn't fit his thigh, and was probably as much use as a chocolate fire-guard. But it's the gesture, right?

Motivated by my guilty conflicting thoughts, I asked if I could pray with him before he went. He said, 'Yes, do that now.' I now felt commanded to pray for him. I felt my words dry up – choked with guilt, anger and confusion. My first line was, 'Bless this man on the road' (long pause, perhaps felt as meaningful). My second line was, 'Bring peace to his heart as he travels' (even longer pause, more embarrassing than profound). Amen.

I was so uncomfortable with Elijah AND the uncharitable feelings I was having towards him.

It's not good theology to cover discomfort with a prayer.

He left without looking back. Unlike myself. Is Elijah a riddle to solve or a koan to ponder? Is Elijah a mystery to un-fathom or a person to forget? Is this what peace-work does to people? I wondered. What had it done to me? Long nights, lost weekends, death threats, domestic absence, debt. As I have reflected on this episode, what comes into view is the pattern that when I am hospitable, I expect things in return – gratitude – expressed gratitude, not hidden. I also expect to feel good at having 'been hospitable', but this had been a strain, a discomfort. And yet we are called to welcome all, not just those who fit our categories of kindness and care. We welcome the strange, and sometimes it feels strange, alien. Elijah was an alien.

And I am also reminded of the times when I hoped that the epic would cover the everyday: the extravagant flowers after the long absence; the bold pronouncements instead of the steady and hidden relationship-building. And the epic ache I felt would be salved by 'sorting other people out', fixing the world and calling it a passion for justice.

Onward, to the inner peace where it all begins, before the action emerges, in whatever form …

~

06. Pure

I am talking about my family background to 12 new volunteers, half of whom are listening in a second language. After an hour, one Catalan volunteer interjects, confused: 'Paul, can you explain how you came from a pure neighbourhood?'

What is he talking about? Who describes their area as pure? I was simultaneously horrified and tickled. This is what came out of my mouth next, in a series of fractured sentences.

'No.'
'I mean, Yes.'
'I mean …'
'When I say the word P-O-O-R,

my accent is making you hear
the word P-U-R-E.'

The Catalan's eyes widened with recognition. The Palestinian smiled, understanding.

As an experiment, I tried saying the word 'poor' in an American accent. All the volunteers laughed and got the meaning. The Catalan volunteer wondered if I could speak all the time in an American accent. No. Another international volunteer asked if I could spell the most important words.

'But what are the most important words?' I asked.

~

07. Yael

Even for a seasoned facilitator, the sight and sound of repeated giggling from a group member can be disconcerting. Overt chuckling was happening in the midst of my talk to new volunteers about the history of Corrymeela. I was mentioning that the Moyle Training Room (where we were sitting) was named after the local geographic region of Moyle. But the giggling kept on bubbling up, infecting others who laughed at others laughing. I was not consciously telling jokes. I subtly checked my trousers. All zipped up.

I checked the flipchart for obvious misspelling of words I had written. None. I narrowed the source of the mirth to one person. It was Yael, a wonderful New Yorker with an explosive laugh. I had to ask her to explain.

Paul: 'Tell me, Yael, you seem amused by something. Is this something you can share with the group?'
Yael: 'Well, you know when you talk about the region of Moyle?'

Paul: 'Yes.'

Yael: 'Well, that's funny.'

Paul: 'Why?'

Yael: 'Well' (giggling again) 'in the Jewish tradition there is the same sounding word: Moyle. But do you know what that means in the Jewish tradition?'

Paul: 'Tell the whole group. They might find it interesting.'

Yael: 'Well, a Moyle, spelt M-O-H-E-L, is a person who ... (more giggles) who cuts off the foreskin of Jewish baby boys when they are just born.'

The word 'foreskin' was creating quite a stir. Someone listening in a second language wanted to know what a foreskin was – they were told. The volunteer, enlightened, nodded sagely. A female volunteer screwed her face up in mock horror. A male volunteer slowly crossed his legs. Then uncrossed them. Then crossed them again.

Yael: (laughing loudly) 'So, whenever you have been mentioning Moyle, another image has been coming to my mind.' (more giggles) 'I'm sorry.'

Paul: 'So, the Moyle Training Room is the Male Circumciser Room?'

Yael: (shrieking) 'Exactly!'

One word. Several meanings. Mystery solved. And a model for good reconciliation practice: how to hold lightly (and measure accurately) the different meanings for the same thing. And now the Moyle room has been forever transformed for me by an encounter with another tradition.

Snip.

~

08. Welcome to community

Today's problem to solve: I am informed that a volunteer has been officially diagnosed with scabies. I project an aura of calm. Inside I am itching with anxiety. I have never been here before – dealing with a person with scabies in a close-knit community.

The official National Health Service (NHS) website says: 'Scabies is very common.'

Not in my world. The very word 'scabies' makes me prickle at the mention of it. I associate it (rightly or wrongly) with dirtiness, scratching and lack of hygiene.

I don't want to catch scabies.

I say (in a comforting tone): 'I have never had to deal with scabies before. I'm sure we can sort this. I will try to contact a community member with medical expertise.' The official NHS website says: 'Scabies is very common, and anyone can get it.'

This fact is jarring my head. I can't get scabies. I'm very clean. I would feel ashamed if I got scabies. The official NHS website says: 'Scabies is very common, and anyone can get it. It should be treated quickly to stop it spreading.' Shit! I need to act fast. I need to phone someone who knows more than I do. I phone a community member who is a GP. She is helpful, casual almost: 'Scabies is common.' (Where do these people live and work?!) She told me what to do: 'Get cream. Use cream. Wash clothes and bed-linen.' Just like that. My head is itching. I am sweating at the thought of what comes next.

With the help of Dustin, one of the Volunteer Support Team, we go to Ballycastle to get cream. Scabies cream. We need enough scabies cream for over 20 people. We buy all the scabies cream in Ballycastle. We order more scabies cream. Just in case. We carry our 'shield and cure' in white plastic bags, hiding the contents from curious spectators. Adding to this pressure is the news that a new volunteer is arriving today. To live in Scabies Central. What are we going to say to her? *Welcome to Corrymeela. There is a scabies scare. We don't practise scapegoating here, but, somebody brought scabies into this community!*

I call a community meeting for all those living (or regularly in) the volunteer house. I explain carefully what has happened. I keep it official and brief. Everyone in the room knows who is unwell. I use clinical language. I do not apportion blame. Everyone present knows who has scabies. I say: 'We all need to use a special cream. We all need to wash our clothes and bed-linen carefully.' In a dead-pan voice I say: 'The NHS, the British Health Service, say, on their official website, that anyone can get scabies.' (Is this helpful? Am I saying – you're next! There is no escape. Nobody is immune!) I say in my dead-pan voice: 'Scabies has nothing to do with poor hygiene.' How are the international volunteers translating this? Scabies rhymes with rabies. And itchy babies. And Hades. Sweet Jesus, who healed the lepers, help me! I have never in my life been more sincere or literal in my prayers.

Dustin stands to one side, holding a flimsy white plastic bag full of scabies cream. Or is it anti-scabies cream? He holds the bag away from his body, as if its contents are contagious. He holds the total supply of scabies cream in the whole of Ballycastle. I am asked lots of technical questions. I speak calmly, slowly. I read what to do off the outer packaging of the cream. I am itching in the groin area. I do not scratch. I tell the volunteers to read the instructions that come with the cream on how to apply it properly. I say: 'Please come' (hoping no one will) 'and talk to me privately if you have any questions you can't ask in a group.' I officially finish the meeting. Volunteers sprint for Dustin and his flimsy bag of salvation. A line then forms in front of me – volunteers with cream in their hands and queries in their heads. I give them what I have. Which is the ability to appear calm and the skill of being able to read off the box that contains the scabies cream. (Later, I will have to go home and tell Joanne the good news: 'Hello, love. I might have scabies. I have to rub this cream all over. All over. Can you help me spread it on?' She will be looking for gloves. And divorce papers.)

Here are the official instructions on how to use the cream. There are ten instruction points and a preamble. I have imagined a space for prayer after each instruction point. What type of prayers? Prayers of courage, strength, patience and resilience. Prayers for the Corrymeela Community. And all those in community who brush hair and shake hands. And all those in community who lean in and listen long, who hug and wrestle and hold and carry. I have written a personal prayer at the end of each instruction point. However, this is merely a guide. Do not feel restricted by my sample prayers if and when you need to administer scabies cream.

The preamble

Do not bath or shower before putting on the cream. Make sure you have been supplied with enough cream or lotion before starting to apply it.

Instruction 01

Remove all clothing. Remember to take off watches and rings. If it is not possible to remove a ring, move it to one side, then treat the skin surface that is normally underneath the ring. Wait for the skin to dry before returning the ring to its normal position.

Space for prayer

Lord, I remove my wedding ring and weep. I feel invaded, reduced, afraid. In this place of No Escape, help me to face this moment as I guide the medicine over my body.

Instruction 02

The cream or lotion needs to be applied to the whole body surface including the scalp (all over the body from head to toe), only avoiding the eye area and inside of the nose and mouth.

Space for prayer

Not my hair, Lord. (Yes. In your hair.)
Not in my hair, Lord. (Yes. In your hair.)

Instruction 03

Squeeze the cream into the middle of your hand or tips of fingers. If a lotion has been prescribed, this is best applied using a small paint or pastry brush.

Space for prayer

Thank you, Lord, that I have cream and not lotion.
A pastry brush is not required.

Instruction 04

Apply to the skin.

Space for prayer

Lord, as I touch the surface of my body, rise up from the deep places of my soul.

Remind me with every rub that there is more than the eye can see. (And keep me from rubbing cream in my eyes.)

Instruction 05

Take special care to get it into all the skin creases of the body, e.g. nipples, scrotum and between the buttocks. Particular attention needs to be paid to the skin between the fingers and toes, under the nails and behind the ears. You will need someone to apply the cream or lotion to your back.

Space for prayer

What a blessing it is, to have someone to call on to apply scabies cream to the hard-to-reach areas of my back. Today my prayers will intentionally and appropriately include the words nipple, scrotum and buttocks.

Instruction 06

Let the cream or lotion dry before getting dressed or it may rub off. This takes 10–15 minutes.

Space for prayer

Standing naked doing nothing but enduring, when I could be accepting an education.
What can I learn from being this exposed?

Instruction 07

Do the soles of your feet last after the body treatment has dried. This is best done with your feet resting on top of or dangling over the side of the bed.

Space for prayer

Lord, I have never minded my feet. Thank you for my feet. Let other parts of me that I find unacceptable come into the Light, be received, welcomed, not hidden or excluded, ignored or rejected.

Instruction 08

Do not bath or shower during the treatment period.

Space for prayer

Lord, give me patience in the mess.

Instruction 09

Put more cream or lotion on any body parts that you may have to wash, e.g. hands, during the treatment period. Depending on the treatment used, this may be for up to 24 hours after first applying the cream or lotion.

Space for prayer

Lord, help me live with paradox. I clean my hands, then administer the cream on to my clean hands, making them feel un-clean, grimy, tainted. This is my defence against scabies.
Lord, help me live with paradox.

Instruction 10

Application of the cream or lotion is best done in the evening.[6]

Space for prayer

Lord, I'm out of words. Hear my silence.

I did not check how people applied the cream to their bodies. They did not tell me. I never want to be told. What I wanted to be told was this: there are no more cases of scabies. There were no more cases of scabies. What I wanted to be told was this: you will never have scabies at Corrymeela ever again. No one could guarantee this. Welcome to community.

Later, in the evening of this long day when I spoke of scabies and handed out cream, a new volunteer arrived. She had signed up for two years. She was excited to be here at Corrymeela. She was looking forward to living and working in community. She was welcomed, shown her room, given a tour. She was given an outline of her induction, and what the next few days would hold. Finally, she was told this: here is a tube of cream. It's so you don't get scabies. The instructions are on the box. Welcome to living in community.

~

09. A Parable

The priest smiled. It was a Sunday morning, and the church where he served was empty. At this time last week there had been 80 people in the pews. Quite a change. Today, instead of people in pews there were small brown paper collection pockets. Some of them looked full. Money on the pews – offerings left by the congregation from the week before that had not reached the collection plates.

The priest knelt and wept for joy.

Last week he had given a short homily on a passage in Matthew's Gospel.

Matthew 5.23–25 says: 'Therefore, if you are offering your gift at the altar and there remember that your brother or sister has something against you, leave your gift there in front of the altar. First go and be reconciled to them; then come and offer your gift.'

What if his congregation never came back? What if his church building stayed empty?

Then he would know that his work had been fruitful. Then he would know that his people were still faithfully walking the road of reconciliation.

~

10. Lift

One morning I had no car to take my youngest daughter to school. I was stuck.

I went down to the centre to see who was about. I didn't want to abuse my power.

I didn't want to blur the boundaries as to what I could and couldn't ask the staff.

But mostly, I didn't want to appear needy. But, I *was* in need. I didn't like to ask for help.

But, I needed help. Reluctantly, I approached one of the Corrymeela staff (a housekeeper) to see if she could help me out with a school run. 'No bother,' she said. 'Get the child and let's go.'

As I ran back up the road to the house and a waiting daughter, I mused on the generosity of this staff member, and about how little I knew about her. She was quiet. She never attended morning worship/reflection (unless compulsory). She seemed uncomfortable in large meetings. She was local. She was a grafter. (Not exactly an encyclopaedic knowledge of the person.)

I gathered my daughter and we ran down the hill to our lift. No sooner were Lucy and I in the car and seatbelted when this normally word-shy housekeeper started to talk. And talk. All the way along the coast road to school. All the way back from school along the same narrow coast road, cliffs on the right, sea on the left. Talking about near-death experiences, about her business shrewdness, about her family, about her animals, about her plans for the future. I had never heard this person speak so much. I was confused. Why now? Her turf? Her in the driving seat? Her decision? And me in the passenger seat. Buckled in. Being driven. A man in need. A parent in difficulty.

We got back to the centre and I said: 'Thanks for everything.' And she said: 'Thank you. For letting me drive you. Any time.'

~

11. Happy Monday

Every Monday morning we begin in the Croí. It's a 9.30 am start, and all the volunteers know they are to attend. It's the only compulsory worship time of the week. Other events are encouraged, but this one is underlined. So, every Monday, I lead the community: staff, volunteers, community members. I choose the music which plays as people enter and wait. I nod at each entrance. On each chair a book has been placed: *Travelling the Road of Faith* – a collection of prayers, songs, reflections. On the table: a lit candle, an open Bible, a turf cross. I formally welcome the room. I inform people new to this space and ritual what we are about to do. I offer a Gathering Prayer, often this one:

Creator Spirit, be with me
As I enter the stillness where you wait for me

Spirit of Christ, live in me
That I may receive the gift of your peace

Holy Spirit, open my ears
And help me to listen.[7]

I unfold the prayer slowly, trying to let go (of past and future plans) and open up to what the moment holds, with a plan in my hand and more than this day's weight on my shoulders.

We perform this ritual in the same way every week, with only occasional variations. How does it stop from becoming repetitively dull, tired or lifeless? Well, breathe in. Hold the breath. Breathe out. And again, breathe in. Hold. Breathe out. And repeat. A repetition full of life. How then to find and nurture the life in a weekly ritual?

For me, two ways. First, I take the ritual seriously. I believe that the Divine has a plan for this space. And if I stumble in my prayers it doesn't matter. And if I don't always know the plan, I prepare anyway, in faith. Second, I look for food, manna, to nourish my own soul, seeking to scoop a thimble-awareness of the Big-God-Love available for all. I find this in daily practices of reading, silence, service, prayer, encounter, thanksgiving.

Many in the room would not present as having an explicit Christian faith practice. What do they do during the prayer bits? Recognize that it's important to the community they are part of. Know that they are not being forced to believe. Know that they are invited to be part of and can contribute to the gathering. For some it's an exercise in resilience: being present to what they don't believe in or practise. Staying in relationship with people who have deeply different beliefs and world-views. Every Monday morning. For some it's a painful 15 minutes, as the symbols and language used are the same as those used by former abusers. It's hard not to twitch when certain words usher in unholy ghosts, memories of pain and panic.

Other responses I have heard:

'This is intellectual rubbish!'
'Childish nonsense.'
'What would my atheist father say?'
'What would my Imam think?'
'What would my Rabbi disagree with?'
'What would my tribe make of this?'
'Here is another new false god.'
'God, rid me of God ...'
'Why can't he speak in Spanish/Arabic/German/Dutch/
Swedish?'

And it's a Monday morning, and tiredness is spread around the room, and the week ahead is looming.

A small space in the ritual is created for optional reflection. Sometimes this is filled with silence. Sometimes it's a song, an action, a thought, a reminder. Once, I brought in some freshly dug soil and placed in on the table beside the cross, Bible and candle. And I said:

'This is the dirt of life. We all share the same planet. It's not equally shared. Take turns (if you can) to put your hands into the dirt. Feel its coolness, its texture. This is life: messy, hard to contain. Put your hands in the dirt.' (Several people declined!)

Then it's back to the structure. I say: 'Let us remember the greater Corrymeela Community by reading from the Daily Prayer Guide. I will read the list of those mentioned on that day. We will pause and remember.'

Then I say: 'We end our time of worship by reading together a litany for our staff and volunteers.' This litany:

Leader   We give thanks to God for all staff and volunteers here – for our work, our dedication and our support for the whole programme of Corrymeela.

	We hold in our thoughts and prayers all volunteers, administrative, catering, housekeeping, maintenance, gardening and programme staff.
All	Help us to remember that, while we have different tasks, we are working for a common purpose.
Leader	Our work is often difficult and we live with many stresses and tensions.
All	Help us also to celebrate the joys and share the sorrows that we experience within our community.
Leader	We give thanks for those who work with hands and with heads
All	for those who lead and those who listen
Leader	for those who cook and wash
All	for those who clean and scrub
Leader	for those who type and copy
All	for those who handle figures and finance
Leader	for those who plan
All	and those who support
Leader	for those who buy and sell
All	for those who dance and sing
Leader	for those who cut grass and repair leaks
All	and those who worry behind the scenes
Leader	for those who bring groups and struggle with their problems
All	for those who answer the telephone and welcome visitors
Leader	for those who lead discussions
All	and those who make and bring in the tea

Leader	for those who handle cover duties
All	and those who are quietly available when they are needed
Leader	for those who worship and pray
All	and those who doubt
Leader	for those who are enjoying life and for those who are feeling the strain
All	we give thanks. Amen

We then finish with what would traditionally be called the Sign of Peace, typically given with a handshake or a hug, and a phrase of recognition. Something like: 'Bless you. Good Morning. Good to see you. Hello (the person's name). Peace be with you.'

And a mutation of this was the phrase, 'Happy Monday!' And so, the Happy Monday Hug came into being. Criticized by certain religious types for not recognizing their designated source of blessing. Criticized by those who didn't like to be hugged. Criticized by those resistant to anything communal. Criticized by those from a tradition that did not allow hugging between the genders. Praised by the secularists who loved physical contact. I loved making connections at the beginning of the week – trying to gauge the state of a person from their stare, from how they come in for the hug or handshake, and noticing rather than judging whatever way they welcomed me: with a shrink; with limp arms; with a sideways caution, groins never near; with a rib-crushing aggression; with a walking out before they can be touched; with a wide welcome smile; with a wet-face and sorrowful slump; with a polite arm's-length handshake; with a pulled-in-close hug and a whispered 'Bless you.'

Corrymeela has been criticized for promoting an over-bearing 'hug-culture'.

It's easy to see why. We model hugging. We invite people to talk about their feelings. We talk about 'going deeper'. We encourage relationships. Hugging? Sharing feelings? Going deeper? Building relationships? No wonder certain cultural and religious boundaries clash. No wonder it can be taken for something more than friendship. Bodies touching. Whispered words. Strong connections. We try to be explicit about the power of romantic or sexual relations, stressing the personal, interpersonal and systemic impacts. It's not easy to live and work in the same environment. It can both accelerate personal growth and bring an awareness to existing cracks. And sometimes it's a place where old habits and painful grooves emerge.

And sometimes it's a place for healing.

Happy Monday!

~

12. Apart (a part)

Meanwhile,
three hundred yards from
the world-famous
Corrymeela Peace Centre,
in a bungalow
owned by Corrymeela,
Joanne, also known as 'the wife of the Centre Director',
sets the table
for three. Again.
Her two daughters sit down for dinner.
The youngest says:
'Where's Daddy?'

ENCOUNTER

01. Handshake

First-day nerves: my two o'clock appointment on day one as Centre Director is with Martin McGuinness – Minister for Education, Sinn Féin leader. Former IRA member. Hate figure in my family when I was growing up. It is not my first time meeting a member of Sinn Féin or a former member of the IRA, but it is my first-time meeting Martin. Thankfully, the out-going Centre Director was doing a handover with me, and was still around to organize the initial greetings and a tour of the site. Am I allowed to feel a little overwhelmed at this early point in this long day of firsts? My therapist would later reframe this question: *are you allowed to feel what you are feeling? Is that what you are asking? Maybe a better question might be: how do I feel about what I am feeling?*

Ashamed, happy, content, legitimate? Or perhaps another question: who decides what are acceptable or unacceptable feelings?

I remember a line of people excitedly waiting for Martin in the reception area of the main building – a mix of staff, volunteers and community members. Martin smiled and slowly shook hands as he walked the line. He was now well-rehearsed at this line-traversing. About halfway through the welcome line I saw a thing: one woman putting her hand out then dramatically removing it before it met Martin's outstretched hand. She had made her point: *I may be part of this line, but I don't have to shake your hand.*

Martin nodded, acknowledged her, walked on to the next person. He knows he is not welcome everywhere. But in Corrymeela? And on my first day as Centre Director? Sure, what's in a handshake? Why be impolite and unwelcoming? A burst of fragmented thoughts combusts my head – voices I grew up with, worked with, worked against: I know where your hand has been. I think I know where your hand has been – on triggers, fuses, making signals of approval for the killing and maiming of others. I know a man who can't shake your hand because he has no hand to shake, having had his hand forcibly removed for the purposes of creating a United Ireland. A United Ireland made of body parts. A Frankenstein country built on the dead.

On my first day as Centre Director I shake hands with many people, including Martin McGuinness – Minister for Education, Sinn Féin leader. Former IRA member. Hate figure in my family when I was growing up. And today, I am the Centre Director of Corrymeela – a place where people are welcomed, and are welcome to shake or refuse to shake the hand of their enemy.

As the Corrymeela tour continued that day (my first day) we had been allowed into a session which comprised a variety of ethnic groups from across the world. A Zulu circle dance was about to begin. Martin smiled as if this was what he did most Mondays.

Watch a Zulu circle dance where you counted and jumped

one
two
three

four
five
six
seven
times.

And then the plucky facilitator takes Martin by the hand and invites him into the circle, to join in with the many nations dancing and counting. And he did. Join in, sweat appearing on his brow as he counted and jumped

one
two
three
four
five
six
seven
times.

I like what I see of this man so far. Lord, grant me discovery beyond but not obscuring a person's history, allegiances and actions.

And then, in June 2012, Martin becomes (for some) a reconciliation symbol, by shaking hands with the Queen of England, Elizabeth. What a risk, what a day. Where a handshake doesn't fix everything, but helps to light the way for other work.

Lord, grant me discovery beyond but not obscuring a person's history, allegiances and actions.

~

02. David

A few weeks before he died (no one knew how long he had left), a Corrymeela community member said to me, 'Time is running out for David.' I found a phone and made an appointment to see him two days later. I had presented the meeting on the phone to David as a chance for me to talk over some issues about Corrymeela. I had asked if he was OK about this, as he was still officially 'off the clock', not at work. His monotone voice gave nothing away. As usual. David annoyed many people with his lack of gush and with his no-hug policy. If you wanted someone to say sweet nothings at a social event, David was not your man. Apparently, at his interview for Leader of Corrymeela, in both a confession and clarification, David had bluntly and unapologetically said, 'If you want a touchy-feely pastoral person for Leader, I am not the right person. That's not me.' I hope that story is true. It's very 'David'.

I turned up outside his tiny semi-detached house in South Belfast, carrying biscuits and foreboding. And a small list of work questions. As I sat in the car outside, I prepared myself. I was used to being with people in pain. But I was upset at David's state of health and so was struggling with my own angst. I ran through things I might share about the centre, and things I would not bother him with. I resolved to stay for an hour, not to be a burden, to attend to whatever needs were presented. If David was true to normal form, he would go down my list with a cool precision, and create a set of actions ranging from 'Save it for next time, leave it for now' or 'deal with this first'. 'Save it for next time.' Charged words in this context. I made one more decision. I wanted to meet David physically. I wanted to meet more than his mind. I wanted to touch him. I had no rationale for this, and this was not the expectation of our usual encounters. I knew hugs were off the agenda, and with his walking stick and declining strength, perhaps even a handshake would be too much.

Perhaps a friendly hand on his shoulder? (He's not a dog to pat, *there, there*.) I need to remember this is not primarily about my needs. Good to register my needs, but they come second to David and his preferred arm's-length distant style.

I ring his door-bell, unclear as to how to be physical with a man who was dying and who resisted physical contact. I wait. Nothing. I don't want to ring again, so I listen. No sound of Mathilde (his wife) saying 'I've got it' in her still-Swiss accent after all these years living in Belfast. No sound of a limping David, clanging up the hall with his walking stick. I wait. Still nothing. I listen. Nothing. I ring the door-bell again and wait. This time I hear a shuffling in the hall, inner doors opening, more shuffling. David opens the door in his too-big threadbare jumper and falling-off-his-hips corduroy trousers. I will try for a handshake. I reach out to formally shake his hand. He stretches his hand out, grabs my hand weakly, and at the same time, shockingly, pulls me into his body for a close body hug. And more, he adds to his gentle hug a big slobbery, beard-rough kiss on my cheek. David Stevens has pulled me in close for a hug and a kiss? What on earth was going on?

He welcomed me in with a smile. 'It's good to see you', he said, sounding like he really meant it. We sat in the back living-room. The floor was covered with small pieces of white paper, type on the front, David's scrawls on the back. Recycling old notes. His undecipherable hand-writing had deteriorated even more since his illness.

Books by Simone Weil, James Alison, Rowan Williams littered the floor. His modest and (to my taste) tasteful art collection make potent imagination-windows on the plain walls of his house. (I see both a Sean Scully print and a Jonny McEwen painting that I particularly like.) We sit surrounded by words on paper at our feet. We smile at each other, like two teenagers who have gotten away with stealing apples from an orchard and are wildly happy in this secret complicity.

I don't know where to begin.

David is still the leader of Corrymeela. David is my supervisor, so we are ostensibly here to talk about work. I don't know where to begin. David knows. David knows he is dying and so he begins with poetry. 'I have written some poems.' I didn't know David wrote poems. 'Would you like to hear them?' It can be stressful listening to someone else's work. It's an intimate thing – to share what you have written. It's even more intimate when there's just two of you. I knew and admired David's prose, but I had never read or heard any of his poems. I feel honoured and afraid. What if it's awful? I will fake appreciation. 'Yes, I'd love to hear some poetry,' I say, in response to his request to be an audience for his poems. David weakly leans down to the floor and picks up a few sheets of paper. He coughs and begins to read …

I cannot remember a single word. I have a vague recollection that the subject matter was mortality. And love. I remember us weeping. Weeping and staring at each other's faces as we wept – over poetry, over life, over loss, over and over. David is dying. Was this poetry always there? Was it the side-effect of a medication? Was it a disinhibition brought on by the illness? Was this always a part of David – lyrical, tender, flooded with feeling? Or was this another David, a new David, a last David? I want to know but it doesn't matter. All that matters is the 'being present'. Sitting with the poems of a dying man. Trying to avoid the clichés. Trying to turn feeling into words or to be silent.

Non Clamor, sed Amor, psalit in aure Dei.
(Not Noise, but Love, makes music in the ears of God.)
Thirteenth-century Catholic liturgy

~

03. Plastic bag

We had never met before. A lady from Dublin and her plastic bag. Late sixties, dyed blonde hair, large-voiced. She had arrived at the centre with a person I did know, a trauma expert who had wanted a place to rest for a few nights. And the chance to chat about possible work with Corrymeela. The trauma expert, not the Dublin lady, was the reason why, at 8 pm on a Friday night, I was sitting trading stories with the two of them, at the wooden dinner tables in the main house. The Dublin lady was a friend of the trauma expert. The trauma expert was serious and sober. The mystery blonde was playful, joyous and full of stories. She talked about her son. 'He's a musician,' she said. 'He plays guitar,' she said. 'He writes his own songs,' she said. Mothers love to boast about their sons. I imagined a twenty-something bloke, still living at home with his mum, haltingly strumming his way through a version of 'Whiskey in the Jar'.

'He was in a wee film as well,' she said. 'Great,' I said. 'He doesn't touch the drink,' she said, 'on account of his da touching it too much. Teetotal he is.' 'OK.' 'He was in that film … *The Commitments*. Have you heard of that one?' I loved that film. Such swaggering swearwords. And such great soul tunes. I expected her to say he was an extra or something.

'And then he was in that other wee film: *Once*. Have you seen it?' This was one of my favourite films of recent years. 'Who was he in the film?' I asked. 'The star,' she said. 'I'm Glen Hansard's mum.' Glen Hansard's mum?!

'He got the Oscar for best song for that film.' I knew. 'He was awful pleased as punch he was. I was so proud of him. You know he got Tom Jones to send me a birthday card? Now there's a singer,' she said. 'Tom Jones. I love a crooner.' I was talking to Glen Hansard's mum. I'm trying not to smile *too* much. I am a mega-fan of Mr Glen Hansard. 'And he does these busking fundraisers every year for a homeless charity in Dublin. In Grafton Street. And he gets his friends to play with him.' He gets his friends to play with him? 'Bono came to see him and sang a few tunes. I don't care what people say about Bono, but he's got a big heart. Not fussed on his music. And at the end of the session, do you know what he did, what Bono did?' Fire himself from a cannon? Turn water into wine? This conversation was leaving me totally unable to predict who would walk into the next scene. 'He throws a cheque into the hat gathering coins. How much for? I'll tell you: 20,000 Euros. People say Bono is just an ego on legs. I don't really know what that means. All I know is the cheque didn't bounce and that's 20 grand to a good cause.'

I can usually hold a poker face, keep my feelings masked. But tonight, I am melting before this Dublin stranger who is fast becoming my favourite person ever from Dublin. Apart from Glen Hansard and Bono. And James Joyce. We talked on. The trauma expert looked bored. She's maybe heard these stories before. It's hard to get serious chat going when you are talking about Glen Hansard, Tom Jones and Bono. We pour more tea. I have a few stories myself, but at the moment I am happy to be warmed by these surprising celebrity-strewn tales. I smile and listen and nod. I am happy to be in the presence of this woman, who arrived a stranger, clutching a plastic bag containing her essentials for staying a weekend.

'I'm very proud of my Glen. Very few people get to win an Oscar.' What an understatement. 'Would you like to see it?'

'See what, now?'

'The Oscar.'

'You have a picture of it?' She smiles at me, pauses, then reaches down to get a picture of her son with his Oscar. She loudly explores the plastic bag on the floor at her feet. And then she did it. She pulled out *the* Oscar. Glen's Oscar. She had been carrying an Oscar in her plastic bag.

It's an Oscar. An actual Academy Award for the song 'Falling Slowly' from the film *Once*.

'Who wants to hold it?' she said.

We held it. We posed with it. We had our photos taken with it. Not many people have held an Oscar. Not many people have been this close to an Oscar.

At Corrymeela we welcome unexpected gifts in plastic bags. How do you prepare for unexpected gifts in plastic bags? Like this:

You say, 'Hello.'
You show the person to their room.
You get them food.
You make them tea.
You make them more tea.
You say, 'You can make tea any time you like.'
You show them round the site.
You give a welcome speech.
You say, 'You are welcome.'
And then you show you mean it.

And then you wait.
Wait to see what happens next.
Open to expectations being exploded or shrunk.

We welcome people and their baggage. We don't ask what's inside. But we weigh each situation with curiosity and grace.

~

04. Country kids

Ten male teens from a rural village. Ranging in age from fourteen to seventeen. Their first time at Corrymeela. Country, not city, kids. On the edge of things. Still at home but on the run from the itching family circle. Bored, bristling with teen-roar-energy, innovative at finding mischief. 'Known' by the local police. They have the run of the village – bolting from small shops where the crisps bags bang and pelting down back-entries, panting, laughing. They are visible because they play outdoors. They are labelled 'loud' when they talk outdoors after 9 pm about football and fantasy sex.

It is their first time at Corrymeela. For most of them it's their first time being away from home without parents. Two youth leaders with them. One they know well. The other is new. 'Newbie' is being introduced to them for the first time at this residential. They are scheduled to stay Friday night through to Sunday afternoon.

This is also a first for one of the new Corrymeela volunteers – their first big residential. The volunteer says she wants to work with young people, that she loves young people. This may change after working with *actual* young people.

'You are very welcome', says the duty manager, giving the compulsory speech for each new residential group.

The country kids are twitchy, look distracted. They appear not to be listening to the explanation about the boundaries of staying at Corrymeela: no alcohol or drugs, the residential units being closed-up at midnight; smoking guidelines; fire procedures. It's not a fun list. And, delivered in the wrong tone, it can also sound like a list of threats. But the point of the speech is to offer a welcome, supplemented by a list of guidelines about how to be a temporary part of our community.

It's Friday night: 8 pm. The kids are cagey and restless in a strange place. I head home for an evening with the family.

Saturday morning: 10 am. I am on a rare off-day. My off-days are precious, but I am contracted as the Person To Contact if there is an untoward incident. My mobile rings. It's work. There has been an untoward incident involving the country kids.

I choke down my last piece of toast and give Joanne an unwelcome buttery-crumb kiss.

Joanne is used to her Saturdays being disrupted. She does not disguise her impatience at this inconvenience. We have spent an hour together in the last six days. The kids are still asleep or not out of their rooms. Family is currently being anchored by Joanne.

I walk down the hill, gazing at Rathlin Island in the distance, its beauty lost in my preparation for what I am to meet at the centre.

The country kids had been bold boys in the night-time. A fire extinguisher had been set off, creating a white Christmas feel in October. Foam on the furniture. A dent in the red extinguisher. It's an exciting thing to set off a fire extinguisher. The country kids had also thrown tea-bags at a white wall, making a drippy-brown Jackson Pollock impression. The volunteer who loved working with young people was looking pale. This was not what she had imagined – feeling so out of control, so power-less. *The kids have the power* was her experience.

I spoke to the duty manager and got more of the picture. One of the youth leaders, the one they knew, was leaving their youth club. He had told them this last night. An adult they trusted was leaving their world. And presenting a replacement, who didn't know the kids from Adam. Might this have something to do with their behaviour? And did motivation matter? The extinguisher *had* been let loose. The tea-bags *had* hit the wall and a poignant backstory would not clean up the mess. Apparently, the departing youth leader was deeply apologetic at his group's behaviour. I asked the duty manager and vol-unteer to pass on that I was now aware of the situation, that I was on-site, and that I would be monitoring the group's progress. That they were very welcome to stay at Corrymeela IF they could keep within the bounda-ries outlined. Another volunteer listening in burst out, 'They should just be asked to leave. Pack up. Go. They shouldn't get away with such bad behaviour.' I asked the volunteer to leave it with me, thanked her for her views, and told her not to repeat what had happened, or her opinion of what needed to happen. I didn't want this group to become the most exciting thing on the site. There can be a toxic curiosity about transgression and transgressors. We try, at Corrymeela, to work creatively to eradicate the binary of 'goodies and baddies', while at the same time keeping everyone accountable and respon-sible for their actions.

I made a cup of tea and made myself visible and available for conversation, trying to exude a calm and approachable authority. On quite a few occasions it has been said to me, sometimes in a joke, that all I do as Centre Director is sit drinking tea and chat to people. That it's not real work. And here I am, on a Saturday morning, laughing at jokes, telling stories, looking like nothing is going on, with not a hint that, simultaneously, someone else is completing an untoward incident form about the night before.

By lunch-time another incident had occurred with the country kids. My lunch was interrupted to tell me this. Soup can be re-heated. This incident involved a cliff.

Corrymeela is situated on a cliff. The road from the coast snakes narrowly up the hill, and when you arrive you don't always know how high up the site is. The duty manager mentions the cliff as part of the welcome speech. If it's a family group with young kids, or a school group, then the fact of the cliff is stated bluntly: Stay away from the edge! For adults, a joke is made of the fact – we haven't lost anyone yet from falling off the cliff, but do be careful, especially at night in the dark. This often gets a nervous laugh from listeners. For youth groups the cliff gets a mention as something dangerous. But not too dangerous. If it's hyped too much then it can become the most attractive place to visit. 'Let's go and look at the dangerous cliff. Let's get really close to the edge.' It's the Don't Walk On The Grass phenomenon. You don't want to walk on the grass until you see the sign.

The Cliff Incident: four country kids had gone exploring. Not all of the group, but part of the group. The view they saw from their piece of cliff was of Rathlin Island – five miles away. It doesn't look five miles away. Strangely, it sometimes looks close enough to hit with a stone. It is impossible to hit it with a stone from this distance. Directly below their cliff-view is a steep drop into bushes, then the public road where cars drive up and down at regular intervals. The road is certainly within stoning distance. Then there is the caravan park, at the bottom of the hill. And from their cliff-view the country kids would have seen the flat metal roofs of caravans corralled in a row. Then it's the sea. Not far, but too far to hit with a stone. Even by an Olympic athlete.

The fab four from the youth group had seen all of this. They had spotted Rathlin. They had glimpsed the road. They had surveyed the caravan roofs. They had taken in the sea. And then stones had rained from Corrymeela. Missiles from a peace centre.

Some hit the road. No cars were hit. (No cars were passing.) Some stones hit the metal of several caravans. No person had been hit with a stone. Not a single stone had reached the sea. Not a single stone had reached Rathlin. The boys had been spotted by the youth leader and told to stop. The youth leader came and apologized, again, hoping no harm had been caused.

Then another angle on the story of the stoning. From down below. The owner of the caravan site has come up to complain. Straight from the target's mouth. He had been walking on his caravan site when a stone had ricocheted off a caravan roof on to the path he was walking with his dog. The owner of a luxury caravan had burst out of their van to see what was going on – their roof had been hit. Corrymeela!! It had to be Corrymeela!!!

Stones had rained from on high. From that so-called Christian community. We are being stoned by Christians. The owner was very upset. I took him somewhere private and let him vent his tale of woe. A long, conflicted history emerged. Not just this incident, but years of being at the bottom of Corrymeela. Years of strangers walking through his site late at night. Years of people being stoned. He was furious and frightened: someone could have been killed!

I apologized and told him I would investigate and get back to him.

'These people need to go,' he said, not getting out of his seat when I stood.

'They need to stop throwing stones,' I said.

'They can't get a free holiday to throw stones,' he said.

'They need discipline and boundaries,' I said.

'Someone could have been killed,' he said again, with years of worry and anger in his voice.

'Leave it with me,' I said.

I spoke again to the retiring youth leader, relaying the views of the owner of the caravan park. The youth leader was distressed by this and left to gather the group. I stay outside of the room where they are meeting. I don't want to go in just yet. Fifteen minutes later he comes out of the room, flushed and flustered. A variety of reasons for having thrown stones were given:

> 'We were trying to roll stones down the hill.'
> *(Possible but not likely.)*
> 'We were trying to reach the sea.'
> *(Plausible but no excuse.)*
> 'We thought they were gypsy caravans.'
> *(Perhaps told as a bravado joke to deal with nerves.)*
> I felt my anger rising.

The youth leader looked sheepish at this point. He said: 'I am very sorry. The group are very sorry. It wasn't the whole group.' I listened, weighing my options. I didn't want Corrymeela to be a place primarily for well-polished, well-behaved polite kids. Neither did I want people causing damage and acting like there were no consequences. Someone could have been badly injured. Mercy and Justice were wrestling in my head/heart/belly. I waited for the youth leader to finish. He said: 'I asked the group if they felt they could keep to the boundaries and rules of Corrymeela. And they said, "No, we are not able to keep to the rules."' And then his eyes grew moist. 'But they might one day. One day they might be able to keep the rules of Corrymeela.' He continued: 'The group then decided that they were not ready for a residential at Corrymeela, and that they needed to leave …'

I nodded. I told him that the group would be welcome back to Corrymeela if some preparation work was carried out beforehand. I did not want to end with the boys feeling that they were getting a lifetime ban. 'Please come back, under different circumstances,' I said.

The group packed up. The youth leader who was leading but leaving said that we should send him the bill for the fire extinguisher. The group got on the minibus and left. We waved goodbye. Some goodbyes are easier than others. The volunteer who aspired to be a youth worker said, 'That was awful – are all youth groups like this? I didn't know what to do.' I said, 'After the clean-up, let's go and talk about what happened. This could be a great learning experience for us.'

Communities are intricate communication systems. Fired-off fire extinguishers were the talk of the evening at Corrymeela. And tales of throwing stones at vans that might have held 'gypsies'. And this question: who should be allowed to come to the centre? For some, it was a theoretical: 'All are welcome!' For others, it was: 'They can only come if they behave.' (Mercy and Justice wrestling.) For the volunteer who had witnessed the mayhem, who had tidied up afterwards, it was the beginning of self-knowledge – not 'These are bad boys', but rather 'What will I do the next time I feel this frightened?'

On the short walk home after another long day, I wondered if I could have arranged an encounter or some form of communication between the owner of the caravan park and the youths who had thrown down their stones on his livelihood. I wondered if that might have been a healing process. But I didn't know the young people well enough to judge this. And I was too tired for innovative thoughts about restorative justice.

I arrived home and slumped into a comfy leather chair, hoping that I could be invisible (and ignored) for a few short hours. But this was not to be. Children and spouse were waiting for attention, and would not be warded off by stories of stone-throwing country kids. They had their own stories to share.

~

05. From on high

We are waiting to welcome a helicopter from *on high*.

Today is the official opening of the Davey Village, a building named after the founders of Corrymeela, Ray and Kathleen Davey. It is 16 October 2012. We have invited many guests, but only one is coming by helicopter. The guest arriving by helicopter is *not* Liam Neeson, the famous local actor. We had tried to get Mr Liam Neeson to be our special guest. He would have gathered the cameras and shone a light on our cause. We knew someone who knew Liam Neeson. We explored the possibility of Liam attending. The reply we got back was that he was supportive of our work, but that his current schedule made this impossible. Another time, hopefully. However, his mother, Mrs Kitty Neeson, did attend the opening (with her friend), having been invited by the man who was coming from on high via a helicopter (which he was flying).

Kitty was amazing and wonderful, but she did not gather the cameras or publicity. She did, however, know how to 'work a room' and appeared to know all the politicians and VIPs. She seemed very much at home with celebrity and ministers of state, smiling and chatting relentlessly. Kitty's son Liam (who did not attend) was relentless (and in my honest opinion, relentlessly awful) in the *Taken* films. The message behind these films was this: 'For my family, I will kill, shoot, explode, torture anyone.' Many people love these films – it's about protecting your family they say (by killing other families, they don't say). Ah, but sure it's only a story. It's only acting. Just pretend. A pleasant way to pass the time. Watching a violent man kill other violent men. For the sake of a so-called sacred thing – family. And don't we all want to protect our family? Against the baddies. You can't be passive against the baddies. You can't.

This is also the same Liam Neeson, who gave his voice to the mighty Aslan in *The Lion, the Witch and the Wardrobe* movie. Liam was playing the voice of the Lion, Aslan, a kind of Jesus/God representation. What an opening of the Davey Village it would have been if Liam could have roared (like God?) a mighty welcome to everyone. I also seem to remember the Lion had to die in order to end the violence of the White Witch ... he defeated violence by dying, not roaring. By being the lamb.

But society is used to violence being viewed as redemptive. And in an alternative re-imagining of this scene, I picture some cocky youth shouting out to Liam (who, in this fiction, did turn up to the Davey Village opening), after his Aslan impression: 'Here, Liam, do yer *Taken* speech.' (For those who haven't seen the movie, this is the famous scene where Liam is on the phone to the people who have kidnapped his daughter. It is a scene bursting with menace and tension.) But the confident youth, high on celebrity fumes, cannot contain himself. 'Wait,' he says, 'Let me give it a go.' And away he goes, this giddy, good-natured heckler, in a strange American-Irish slur:

'I don't know who you are. I don't know what you want. If you are looking for ransom I can tell you I don't have money, but what I do have is a very particular set of skills. Skills I have acquired over a very long career. Skills that make me a nightmare for people like you.'

The room lights up with laughter. The young eejit, inspired, continues in his stern mid-Atlantic drawl:

'If you let my daughter go now that'll be the end of it. I will not look for you, I will not pursue you. But if you don't, I will look for you, I will find you and I will kill you.'

And what seems like the whole room explodes with laughter at the end of his Liam Neeson impression, and clap their delight at having re-enacted a threat scene from a bloody movie, at the opening of Corrymeela, an open Christian community committed to reconciliation. The Press click and scribble – photograph and make notes on this comedy moment.

However, some in the room have not exploded with laughter, but rather have imploded with rage and hurt and fury at the presumption that this was appropriate at this or any time at Corrymeela, the so-called 'safe space'. Some in the room have borne witness to other types of bomb – have set bombs to kill; have tried to prevent bombs exploding; have caught bombers en route; have had family members maimed or killed.

Not everyone would have laughed at this imagined re-enactment from the film *Taken* in a room *loud* with conversation, celebration and celebrity; in a room *quietly* shouldering lost loves, whispering ghosts, tender wounds, and slow recovery.

~

o6. Covering

It is the opening of the Davey Village, the new residential space at Corrymeela.

Everyone is dressed in their 'very best' and I am struggling with the pomp as I smile about the place in my suave Paul Smith suit (from Oxfam, I proudly tell people). Suited and booted. Shirt and tied. Hats and fancy dresses. I'm trying, but I am struggling not to judge people by their level of sartorial pomp. The more they pomp, the less I seem to rate them. (And someone is coming in a helicopter!) My discomfort is turning into judgement. Of other people in the first instance. But soon I will be judging myself for judging others. Jesus, where are you in the midst of this formal-wear moment? How to get behind the suit, below the surface, further than a name, past the fame (or infamy), beyond the goody/baddy binary temptation?

Speaking of outfits, I once met a man in the Croí who was covered in Jesus. He had somehow gained access to the building before it was locked up at midnight. And now, there he was, a complete stranger, covered in Jesus. He had slept there overnight, covered in Jesus. At the sound of us entering the Croí the next morning he stumbled out to meet us, covered in Jesus. He said, 'Hello, who's in charge? I'm homeless.' Unfortunately, I was in charge, and I was in the middle of a very intense peace conference. And I wanted to know how he had been able to be in this locked building. And I had a thousand things on my to-do list. And where on earth did he get that giant tablecloth with the life-sized full-colour print of Jesus on it? 'I hope you don't mind,' he said, 'I was cold last night and I used this sheet to keep myself warm.' Warmed by Jesus in the lonely night-time. But what's the story beneath his makeshift Jesus duvet? I greeted him, shook his hand, put him in the hands of someone else, came back to him after my 9 am meeting, and started to hear some of the story beneath his makeshift Jesus snuggle-blanket. It took time. But it was easier to listen now that he had taken off Jesus and I had shrugged off my coat of lists.

Speaking of Jesus, a friend of mine once recounted a tale about being on holiday in Paris. He encountered a preacher covered in swearwords. The preacher was arresting, close to getting arrested. He was preaching in the open-air, shouting out his message:

'You all need f**king Jesus. He's the real deal.
He's not a prude.
He's not a killjoy.
He's the f**king real deal.
Don't take my word for it.
I'm a f**king eejit!
Taste and see for yourselves.
Let me pray so you can connect
to the Christ in all,
to the Christ who holds the Universe together.'

'Ephesians was a letter written by a bloke called Paul.
Inspired he was.
Stop and f**king listen.
Are you able to stop for a f**king second?
Listen!
Ephesians chapter three talks about being rooted and established in love.
Now who doesn't want to be loved?
Who doesn't want their f**king lives flowing out of f**king love?
Who?
I f**king do!
Listen to me.'

My friend was stopped in his dirty-sandalled tracks. He had been preached at before. He had been sworn at before. But he had never heard the gospel message laced with F-bombs. Never! Never! Never! Was he stopping because of the swearwords, or because he was hearing the gospel differently in its expletive-shaped frame? My friend was eighteen years old and far from home. He walked on, stirred, confounded, wrapped for a while in thoughts of a strange new world – of gospel glory sparkling with swearwords.

~

07. Past

When and where and how do you start to come to terms with a history where over 3,600 people were killed during the armed conflict in Northern Ireland?

Perhaps here. A single year: 1972. The year I turned eight. The year Mary Peters won an Olympic gold at Munich (my mother looks like Mary Peters).

The year the Shankill Butchers started slaughtering Catholics (my mum is from the Shankill). The year seven IRA internees escaped from the Maidstone prison ship docked in Belfast harbour (my da found this story a hoot). The year of Bloody Sunday and Black Friday (I still can't clean the red from those maps in my head). The year of an IRA Ceasefire (but the guns remained, cocked and loaded). The year 470 people were killed – the worst year for casualties in the Troubles. The year my scout troop did well in the football. I was right-footed and played left back (a year that held more than death).

Say along with me the first ten people killed that year, in 1972:

Keith Bryan

Daniel O'Neill

Peter Gerard Woods

Michael Sloan

Raymond Denham

Maynard Crawford

Eamonn McCormick

Sydney Agnew

Charles Stenford

Peter McNulty

Say along with me the age they were killed in 1972:

Eighteen

Twenty

Twenty-nine

Fifteen

Forty-two

Thirty-eight

Seventeen

Forty

Eighteen

Forty-seven

Say along with me their occupation when they were killed in 1972:

Soldier

Labourer

Publican

Schoolboy

Electrician

Site Foreman

Unemployed

Bus Driver

Soldier

Farmer

In 1972. With a sectarian soundtrack of songs inciting us to take one of two sides. Songs of lament, rage, remembrance. But there were other songs that year, mingling with the soundtrack of blood-rage and mutilation. Blared out from poor-quality radios. Collected on easily warped warm vinyl. Watched religiously on *Top of the Pops*, a three-minute salve of sound.

Say along with me ten song titles from 1972:

'I'd like to teach the world to sing'

'Without you'

'Amazing Grace'

'You wear it well'

'In a broken dream'

'How can I be sure?'

'I can see clearly now'

'Rocket Man'

'Look wot you dun'

'Children of the revolution'

And sometimes liturgies were recited. Like this liturgy that I come back to again and again:

In the midst of hunger and war
We celebrate the promise of plenty and peace.

In the midst of oppression and tyranny
We celebrate the promise of service and freedom.
In the midst of doubt and despair
We celebrate the promise of faith and hope.
In the midst of fear and betrayal
We celebrate the promise of joy and loyalty.
In the midst of hatred and death
We celebrate the promise of love and life.
In the midst of sin and decay
We celebrate the promise of salvation and renewal.
In the midst of the dying Lord
We celebrate the promise of the living Christ.[8]

Liturgies recited together, with closed eyes and open. Not to ward off evil or protect ourselves from feeling. But to hold the feelings true. To find containers that allow (and nurture) the grief and anger and hurt to come out. Not to say, 'It's fine! Jesus is coming!' But to say, 'It's hell and Jesus is here.' To craft a prayer in the gory mess, where the body of Christ is literally being exploded into pieces, and the map of our lives is littered with piss and shit and blood. Where simple answers are not enough to carry the pain and agony. Where ancient texts are wrestled over and thrown away and picked up and prayed out in hoarse voices. Where the term 'reconciliation' is distorted – is 'heard' as surrender, as betrayal of the dead, as a call to shake hands with your enemy/abuser/oppressor. Silence is often the beginning and end of things.

We say the word 'reconciliation' cautiously in the shadow of 3,600 deaths.

Traditions and texts are studied and compared in an effort to find new ways of loving in a time of war. What is it to say in 1972, 'Christ has died, Christ has risen, Christ will come again'? What is it to say in 2019, 'Christ has died, Christ has risen, Christ will come again'? It is to comprehend the war and its casualties. It is to weep with the Creator over a mutilated creation. It is to recognize the war and its origins. It is to cry out and work for justice. It is to be passionate for truth, gentle with our truth claims, open to correction. It is to be graced with new eyes. It is to see our part in the conflict. It is to see 'that of God in every person' (as the Quakers would say). It is to have days where *Christ has died* is the only prayer to accompany the ache. It is to have days where *Christ has risen* seems a ridiculously empty prayer. It is to have days where Christ rises up out of the broken-boned reality of our lives. It is to be sustained in the 'not-yet' of *Christ will come again*. It is to dare. To dare to live as if each moment was a gift from the Creator. A gift infused (in myriad mayhem mixes) with vinegar, sugar, salt and dust. And to give thanks. In the midst ...

~

08. Here, son

'Here, son, I want a word with you.' A gravelly female voice commands my attention.

The owner of the sandpaper speech is smoking outside the front door of the main house. The bus for her departure has just arrived. She is getting a last puff before the journey home. Suitcases are randomly piled near the bus. I had been pointed out by one of the volunteers as The Person In Charge At Corrymeela. 'Here, son, I want to talk to you' is usually a prelude to a complaint. I gather myself to listen, slightly defensive.

She is a woman in her early sixties, dyed blonde hair, dark roots clawing through.

I spot these things – roots – my mother was a hairdresser, was always talking about roots needing to be 'done' and natural hair colours. Not in a critical way, but as the lexicon of her trade. This harsh-tonsilled lady had been part of a respite group – families from challenging social situations needing a break, longing for a different sky.

On the Friday when they arrived, they held on tight to their kids, viewing all the adults with suspicion. By Saturday morning the kids were running full pelt throughout the site, unaccompanied, teetering on the edge of the cliff with excitement. The adults were offered a menu of activities, including massage, arts and crafts, a foot spa, an evening movie. The young kids had a dedicated programme of events. The teens were accompanied to the beach, walked into, not close to, the water, then walked back to the centre, squelchy-happy in their wet trainers and dripping jeans. One young boy never got the knack of being quiet during the moment of silence, and could be heard, every mealtime, whispering loudly about what was on his mind: 'I like carrots! I want Coke! Mummy, open your eyes!'

A few of the families attended the Croí – curious, happy that their kids were made welcome and that no one shouted when a child burnt her finger on a candle. (The first-aid box was opened behind the scenes.) All very pleasant, but what has this to do with peace and reconciliation? If families are faltering, society wobbles. If a community is in chaos, it shakes family. If violence is the highest authority, it creates hard shells and bleeding souls. If communication is distorted, unhealthy conflict emerges.

The respite weekend did not attempt to put their lives in order (whatever that means), did not 'fix' their community, did not solve the 'missing father' theme, did not tell them to stop swearing, did not measure them against their reading ability, did not value them based on their passes in school. We offered rest. For a while. For a bit. For a weekend. We valued each person, encouraged them to find their own dignity. We held them up for a weekend, temporarily shared a piece of their strain. We poured tea and chatted – about sex, drink, food, birthdays, parties. Story after story unfurled, making Corrymeela a richer place for hosting these loud-rude, sad-wonderful, crackling-complex tales.

And this was now Sunday and the group were getting ready to leave. 'Here, son, I want a word with you.' The lady and I sat in the gazebo. She smoked and talked. I watched for signs of an imminent criticism. Most people are grateful and say so. Occasionally there are comments, critiques, complaints. Will it be the food? (Not enough chips.) Will it be the rooms? (I prefer my own bed.) Will it be the programme? (Who enjoys sitting in a circle talking?) Will it be an international volunteer? (That wee foreigner couldn't even speak properly.) Will it be an overly inquisitive community member? (She kept on asking me personal questions.) Will it be a moment in the Croí? (I think there was a Protestant prayer said to God – Jesus!) I waited. Coiled. Hoping I could respond and not react. 'Here, son,' she said. 'Let me tell you something.' And she did. 'When I came here on Friday I hated my daughter (who was also on the trip). And I thought my grandson (also on the trip) was a wee sh*t. I hated my family. I thought – why am I here with people I can't stand? And there's no drink allowed on the site?! Jesus, I thought – I am not going to like this at all. And I thought – Oh God – a new place. What are the rooms gonna be like? What's the food gonna be? What if they get all religious on me? No offence,' she said. 'None taken,' I said. 'I thought – I am a terrible mother. And I have an awful daughter. And I am a monster granny. And now it's Sunday and I have to go home. And now I think this: I was tired out, done. I needed to get away. I love my wee house, but the walls were closing in. And now I think this: my daughter is doing her best. And now I think this: my grandson is hyper but I love him. I needed a break. Thank you. Can I stay?' No. 'Can I come back?'

'You would be very welcome here, if you came again.'

'So, is that a yes? When can I come back?'

'Let's see what we can do.'

She gurgled with amusement, flicked her still-lit cigarette into the grass, and walked towards her luggage and the bus that would take her home. I lifted her smoking cigarette and extinguished it in the nearest sand-filled bucket.

Later that night, my youngest daughter sniffed my hand, as daughters do, and said: 'Your fingers stink of smoke.'

~

09. Notice*

I was too busy to notice, but apparently an uninvited heavily pregnant teen was spotted today at the centre, walking muck from her dirty shoes into the freshly cleaned carpet, quietly singing an offensive song to whoever was within ear-shot, gently brutal, cutting and soothing. How did she get in? And who was going to throw her out? Or was she welcome to stay? Better find the Centre Director.

I was too busy to see her, but a community member I trusted said she heard this: A simple melody. Moving in and out of earshot. Words about being baptized in a sea of scandal, and finding salvation at the heart of that drowning love. Rejoicing in the impossible coming to pass. Talking about a line of mercy passing from generation to generation.

I was too busy to hear, but apparently this pregnant teen with the desert-forged accent took two cups of tea (spilling one) and mumbled as she mingled: about how the divine had scattered the proud; about how the divine had exalted the lowly, graced them with a lover's kiss; about how the divine had filled the hungry, and sent the rich away empty. Where did these things happen? When did these things happen? What does she mean by 'rich'?

A hospitable soul asked her name. The teen mumbled: Mary. She made no sense. Her talk was upside down. She sang of a world disoriented by shocking surprising justice. I was too busy to notice.

* After a dream I had about the Magnificat.

~

10. Limits

Which takes me to the time when I had worked ten days in a row for the good cause of Corrymeela and I had a Saturday off – one day – and then I was scheduled to be back in on the Sunday. So, a precious day, a family day, and our family days are often beach-days, so we took off, we fabulous four, to Portrush and the East Strand and the view of the scraggy Skerries.

I was slowly sand-strolling with my youngest on one part of the walk (Lucy would have been nine at this time). We held hands and traced the line where the sea wet the shore, tempting the waves to baptize our feet. Lu was barefoot. I was in sandals (no socks, you will be glad to hear!). It didn't matter if we got wet, but the game still held us – walk close to the ocean, tempt it with a toe or heel, remove it before it gets licked by a salty tongue of sea. Part of the game was Dad pushing daughter into water, and daughter screeching in fake alarm, and shouting – 'that's cheating! Don't throw me in!' Daughter then proceeds to try and push a weighed-down Centre Director into the wake of the waves. No mean feat after a ten-day stretch of work. But she tried, as children do, to get parents to be present to them, in the wet moment of now.

After this game, we became interested in what was left behind. Left behind by the sea, the wind, by humans. Sticks floated in and floundered on land. Seaweed slinked on the sand. Shells poked shiny-wet out of the sand: beautiful-sad abandoned sea-creature homes. Stones washed smooth and ready to be lifted and held and turned around. And on this particular forage into flotsam, Lucy touched something unfamiliar in the sand with her curious foot. 'What's this, Daddy?' It is a plastic syringe. There is no liquid inside. And no needle. I educate Lucy about syringes. That they are used in hospitals for medical treatments like taking blood and giving medicine. 'I don't like hospitals,' said Lucy. 'Who put it there?' she said. I had no answers. I told Lu about the possible dangers of syringes with needles in them, about how needle-sticks were dangerous, and never to pick one up. 'What will we do with this one?' she said. The syringe is empty. The syringe has no needle. I *could* pick it up. The nearest bin is half a mile away. My daughter is watching. Kids learn from actions more than words. I act. I push the syringe back into the sand. Cover it up with my foot. I say, 'Let's go, Lu.' Lu is still studying the mound where a syringe has been buried by her father. She looks ahead at the stretch of sand. Is she wondering what else is hidden, has been buried by parents earlier that day, last month, 50 years ago?

Lu continues on, finds a flat stone and makes it skim three times on the sea. 'Three times!' she shouts. It is a precious thing to share your daughter's delight at skimming a stone, to see it jump on the water, and to feel your heart leap with the stone. The joy of a skimmed stone.

But this time the joy was struggling to surface. Not for Lu, who was smiling like a Lottery winner. For me. I was still mentally mining the mound of sand covering the syringe that I had covered up, dimming the beautiful sight of my daughter skimming stones with uncomplicated glee. It wasn't my syringe! And I had worked for ten days straight – for God and peace and a peaceful island. My steps were getting slower, my head turning that syringe-moment over and over. The beautiful view was dimming.

One hundred yards into this growing gloom and Lu stops again. More flotsam. Or is it jetsam? Lucy is keeping her curling toes away from this lump in the sand. It's probably something dead. It is a nappy (for American readers, a diaper). It is not an empty nappy. It is a used nappy. It has been filled with poo. Lucy knows exactly what it is. 'What's this, Daddy?' says Lu, wanting me to speak out what she already knew. 'It's a nappy full of poo.' Lucy is in hysterics of giggles. Kids and poo – always a winner in the joke front. 'Who put it there? What are we going to do?' Well, I have already buried a syringe today. What do you do when you're 'done', when your body is 'beat' and you're faced with another decision that seems way too heavy to make. On your only day off after ten days on. On the beach where you want to unwind and not demonstrate ethical living. My daughter is watching. Kids learn from actions more than words. I look around to see if there are any other witnesses. No one looking except Lu. I act ... I pick it up. Lucy shrieks to her mother and sister walking ahead of us on the beach. 'Mum! Alice! Daddy's holding a nappy with poo in it!' I'm sure everyone on the beach within earshot did not look around at this proclamation, but it felt that way. The nearest bin was a quarter of a mile away. I hold the generously filled nappy away from my clothes, hold it out in front of me, and speed up my walking. I am carrying someone else's sh*t. It wasn't me. It's not my sh*t, or the sh*t of my family. But I carry it anyway, to the sound of Lucy giggling and pointing at what I am carrying. I want to make a sign, a disclaimer: 'This is not my poo. This is not my daughter's poo.' But who would believe me? I keep walking, narrow my focus to one thing: get to the nearest bin and dump the dump. After that I can think about ripping all my clothes off and burning them and having a scalding shower for an hour. Finally, I get to the bin at the edge of the path that takes us back to the car. My hand feels radioactive. I reach the car and am handed hand-wipes. I rapidly use six of them. Lucy is smiling as if she is in a Big Smiley Competition and she is about to be crowned the winner. I feel soiled and daunted.

So how did I do in this story? And how did you do, as you read yourself into this story? This story with a backstory of ten days in a row, working too hard, more finely tuned to the needs of others than to my own aches, desires and frailties. I'm not always like this – numbed and desperate for an easy hour of ease. But I'm too often like this – lost for words and weak from making decisions and interventions into lives surrounded by loss, hate, lies and longing. Is this the cost of reconciliation? Am I to become another revered casualty of reconciliation?

> He helped many people – for a good cause.
> He missed his friends – for a good cause.
> He lost his family – for a good cause.
> He lost his health, his mind, his faith – for a
> good cause.

In more lucid moments I see that there will always be more need in the world than any individual can deal with, and that it's not God's plan for us to 'burn out' looking after other people for so-called worthy causes.

Looking out to sea slows me down (if I give it a chance), allows me to experience and embrace the sacred stitches in my life – a weave of relationships with and between Creator (source of all life), creation (the Earth and ALL its inhabitants), self (broken and strong) and spiritual traditions (texts and practices).

Looking out to sea slows me up, reveals the waiting truth that I am a small creature and that the sea is a vast wonder. This waiting truth that whispers (and occasionally bellows) that I am a Beloved being, rising and falling in the sea of Love – in all the shallows and depths of living.

And the Divine Heart pulses out a holy signal-beat:

Beloved
   Beloved
      Beloved
         Beloved

Coda

There are a lot of hugs and handshakes at Corrymeela. We try to welcome people 'as they are', where they are at. We try to discern the many steps and shapes of reconciliation. We also recognize that a handshake is not always the end-goal (transformation is the end-goal – personal, interpersonal and systemic).

Some handshakes are viewed as a betrayal. Some handshakes are regarded as an admission of wrong. Some handshakes take participants back to their childhood: 'shake hands and say you are sorry', as practised in many school playgrounds across the world.

Some handshakes are a first step, a first shake of change. At Corrymeela we ask: how is this handshake progressing the task of reconciliation? Is it helping or hindering the healing process? Some handshakes cannot hold the history of pain. And sometimes, reconciliation is a coming to terms with the fact that the other party does not want to go any further on their journey. And then the reconciliation task is coming to terms with this, allowing this decision to sit in a healthy (and not always pain-free) way with the rest of your life.

Every moment of our lives has the potential for a reconciliation.

We can be quick to judge the loud shouting as wrong. However, it might be the sign of great hurt, a great desire for justice, a deep hunger for right-ness, for righteousness. In saying this, I am not endorsing violent or aggressive behaviour. These things need to be addressed and people held to account. However, conflict does not need to begin or end in violence. And anger is not aggression.

Every moment of our lives has the potential for a reconciliation.

The leg that won't heal (and the learning in the limp). The past that continues to shout loudly (and the search for listening posts). The family in need of respite (and addressing the systems of inequality). The ex-prisoner in need of dignity (and new restorative legal pathways). The outsider brought in (the insider becoming aware of their privilege and power). Education for body, mind, emotion, spirit (fizzy drinks make a terrible breakfast). Scriptures of love embodied (spaces to share precious tales). Enemies humanized (strangers saluted). Prayers learnt, lost and found (waiting in silence for worlds to end, and begin). Risks taken. Violence addressed. Otherness hosted. Tensions held and tested. Discerning the story in every breath. Tea poured. Dishes cleaned. Nurturing communities of celebration, diversity and thanksgiving.

Welcome.

To a life of reconciliation ...

References

1 *Travelling the Road of Faith* – worship resources from the Corrymeela Community (2001), www.corrymeela.org.

2 Ray Davey, *The War Diaries: From Prisoner-of-war to Peacemaker*, Brehon Press Ltd (2005).

3 *The War Diaries*.

4 Michael Stipe, *One Giant Leap – Palm Pictures* (2002).

5 Jean Vanier, *The Broken Body*, Darton, Longman and Todd (1988).

6 www.infectionpreventioncontrol.co.uk.

7 Corrymeela Prayer Guide (2013 version) www.corrymeela. org.

8 *Travelling the Road of Faith*.